The Meaning of Independence

The Meaning of INDEPENDENCE

John Adams, George Washington, and Thomas Jefferson

EDMUND S. MORGAN

UNIVERSITY OF VIRGINIA PRESS   CHARLOTTESVILLE AND LONDON

University of Virginia Press
© 1976 by the Rector and Visitors of the University of Virginia
Preface © 2004 by the Rector and Visitors of the University of Virginia
All rights reserved
Printed in the United States of America on acid-free paper
First published 1976

3 5 7 9 8 6 4 2

LIBRARY OF CONGRESS CATALOGING-IN-PUBLICATION DATA

Morgan, Edmund Sears.
The meaning of independence.
(Richard lectures for 1975, University of Virginia)
Includes bibliographical references and index.
ISBN 0-8139-0694-6
1. Adams, John, Pres. U.S., 1735–1826—Addresses, essays, lectures.
2. Washington, George, Pres. U.S., 1732–1799—Addresses, essays, lectures.
3. Jefferson, Thomas, Pres. U.S., 1743–1826—Addresses, essays, lectures.
I. Title. II. Series: Richard lectures, University of Virginia; 1975.
E322.M85
973.3'13'0922   76-8438

Illustration sources can be found at the end of the book

for J. M. B.

CONTENTS

PREFACE

SINCE WRITING THESE CHAPTERS, I HAVE SOMETIMES WON-
dered what our lives and the lives of these three men would have
been like if the British in the 1770s had acceded to the colonists'
demands and granted them everything they asked for. The British
effectively did that two years after Americans declared independence. The Americans had insisted all along, from 1764 to 1775,
that all they wanted was to have their relationship to the mother
country restored to what it had been in 1763, before the British
began to tax them without their consent. They had said, again and
again, that they did not aim at independence. In April 1778, the
king appointed a commission to proceed to America and offer to
the Continental Congress a suspension of all acts of Parliament relating to America passed since 1763 and any other acts that bothered them. The commission could even propose that royal governors be replaced by popularly elected ones.

It was everything that Americans had asked for and more. It was
everything they had fought for at Lexington and Concord and
Bunker Hill. It was not too little, but it was too late. Two years of
independence transformed Americans. Suddenly and irrevocably
they were a different people. If the British had offered in 1775 what
they did in 1778, we would probably never have heard of the three
men examined here. It had been one of the weaknesses of the
British Empire, perhaps not apparent before 1776, that it had no
room, no imperial offices, open to its colonists. The empire was run
by men whose capacities for doing the job bore virtually no relationship to the archaic processes by which they were assigned it.
Any colonists who might have had the capacities for leading an em-

pire could exercise them only in local politics, an arena insufficiently challenging to command much attention from men of large vision. Independence opened the opportunity for such men to exercise talents that had hitherto lain dormant. Once they moved from private to public, from subject to citizen, from colony to continent, there could be no turning back.

The effect was spectacular. Among the great political figures of American history, by almost any standards, an incredible proportion lived and made their names during the quarter century following independence. Try making a list of great American political leaders and see how few from the nineteenth and twentieth centuries can be found to rank with these three or with James Madison, Alexander Hamilton, and John Marshall. Benjamin Franklin is an exception. He was already seventy years old in 1776. He did not experience the challenge that independence brought to younger men because he had decided long before that future greatness belonged to America and warned his English friends in 1775 that by antagonizing the Americans, "You will only exclude your selves from any share in it." But even Franklin enjoyed the most fruitful experiences of his political career after 1776.

Independence seems not to have brought the same stimulus to the arts that it did to politics. America's cultural independence did not arrive until much later, and its significance and timing are more difficult to assess. But the separation from Britain in 1776 engendered creative political thought and action that have not been equaled since. These three men took part in it. We can be thankful that Britain's generosity of 1778 came too late to stop them.

EDMUND S. MORGAN
New Haven, 2004

JOHN ADAMS

WHEN ENGLAND'S AMERICAN COLONIES DECLARED THEIR independence in 1776, the event could scarcely have come as a surprise to anyone. Long before England had even planted its first colony in the New World, Richard Hakluyt, the most ardent advocate of colonization, acknowledged that Englishmen so far from home might eventually throw off their dependence.[1] It was a commonplace, based on ancient history, that colonies would not forever remain attached to the country that founded them. And by the middle of the eighteenth century English colonial governors and imperial administrators were seeing increasing indications that Americans would one day conform to the classical pattern.[2]

The Americans themselves seem to have been more reluctant than their English brethren to admit the possibility. When the quarrel with the mother country began in 1764, the colonists took pains to accompany their formal protests with affirmations of allegiance. The Stamp Act Congress of 1765 began its declaration of rights with one which asserted "that his Majesty's Subjects in these Colonies, owe the same Allegiance to the Crown of Great Britain, that is owing from his Subjects born within the Realm." The First Continental Congress in 1774 repeated the assurances of loyalty; and in 1775, after the fighting began, the second Congress reassured the mother country, in a statement drafted by Thomas Jefferson, "that we mean not to dissolve that union which has so long and so happily subsisted between us." It would almost seem that independence came as an afterthought to the men who had taken up arms against Parliamentary taxation.[3]

In the light of the colonists' initial reluctance to consider independence, the finality with which they embraced it when it came is a little surprising. By 1778 the English, among whom American independence had for so long been viewed as inevitable, were ready to offer the Americans everything they had asked for if they would forgo independence. But the Americans, who had so recently been disavowing any desire for independence, scarcely gave the offer a serious hearing.[4] Independence, though it would still take a bloody war to achieve, looked more attractive to them than union with England on any terms. What made independence suddenly so desirable? What did it mean to Americans that they should value it above the union that had so long and so happily subsisted between them and England?

I propose to attempt an answer by looking at three men who may fairly be called the architects of independence: John Adams, George Washington, and Thomas Jefferson. Each of them saw in independence a future for himself and for his countrymen that could never be realized in union with England. Each of them was ready for independence before the rest of the country. And each of them perceived the implications of independence with a clarity of vision that few others ever attained. Their visions were not identical, and before their careers ended they had disagreed about a number of things. So, of course, had other Americans. Independence meant many things to many men. I do not pretend that the lives of these three encompassed the whole range of its meanings. Theirs was not the common experience, for they were not common men. But in them we may perhaps see writ large some of the hopes and fears that independence brought to their countrymen.

I want to begin with John Adams, not because he was the most important of the three—for he was not—but because he is the most approachable. It is easier to follow him than the others through the events that transformed British colonists into independent Americans. Having done so, we may be able to approach his two colleagues with more assurance.

We may come upon John Adams first, as another stranger to him did, in 1772. In that year, when the train of events leading to independence was well under way, old William Shirley, former governor of Massachusetts, now retired to his estate in Roxbury, began to hear of the activities in Boston of John Hancock, Thomas Cushing, and Samuel and John Adams. Shirley, who thought he knew Boston politics pretty well, expressed surprise. "Mr. Cushing I know," he said, "and Mr. Hancock I know, but where the Devil this brace of Adams's came from, I cant conceive."[5]

Two years later King George III was only a little better informed. When Governor Thomas Hutchinson stood before him in the summer of 1774, after having been all but driven from his post in Massachusetts by the brace of Adamses, King George was puzzled. "I have heard of one Mr. Adams," he said, "but who is the other?" The Adams that the king knew was Samuel Adams.[6] And two months later when the First Continental Congress assembled in Philadelphia and the brace of Adamses was very much in evidence, Samuel was still the better known and seemed at first the more effective. Joseph Galloway, trying to hold the Congress to a moderate position, found himself defeated at every turn by the superior maneuvering of Boston's most skillful politician.[7] But the Boston politician, skilled as he was in the manipulation of votes, whether at Boston or Philadelphia, was not a man of large vision, not a man to lead others in the formation of a new nation. Samuel Adams remained a dedicated provincial politician, and one suspects that he played a leading role in the First Continental Congress only because its leading business was to bring aid to his particular province. In subsequent meetings of the Congress, his cousin John, a different sort of man, gradually emerged as the more important of the two. John Adams found in the Congress a kind of fulfillment that Samuel never knew, and when the members assembled again after the Battle of Lexington in 1775, it was John Adams who led them patiently but relentlessly down the path to independence. Eventually, of course, he would lead the new nation as president. To understand how someone who seemed in no way remarkable turned into someone who must still be remembered as remarkable is to understand more than a little of what American independence meant to the three men who were most instrumental in bringing it about.

At first sight John Adams would appear almost as limited as his cousin and quite unsuited to the part he played after 1775. That part demanded large vision and imagination, to perceive the needs and dangers that must attend defiance of what was then the world's most powerful country. In order to appreciate Adams's response to the challenge, we need to know his limitations, which were many.

There was, to begin with, something invincibly provincial about him. Though he was widely read, attended Harvard College, then studied law and made his living by the practice of law, though he spent years of his life in France, Holland, and England, his emotional home was his farm in Braintree. He sank the profits from his law practice, which were not great, into buying more land for his farm. He was always daydreaming about it when his mind should have been on more important business. Of course, it has become conventional in our own time for aspiring politicians to insist that they would rather be down on the farm. The surest sign today that a man is a candidate for the presidency is his affirmation that he is not interested in the job but just wants to grow a few tomatoes at his little old place in the country. But John Adams seems almost to have meant it. He was forever writing in his diaries and his letters about the land he was clearing, the stone walls he was building, and the mountains of manure he was acquiring or was going to acquire—especially the last. He had a positive obsession with manure. When he visited Europe later, he took as much pride in the superiority of his own manure piles over the ones he saw there as he did in the moral superiority of his countrymen over the dissolute French and English.[8] No matter where Adams was, he would rather have been in Braintree, gloating over his earthy riches.

In later life when he became president of the United States, he spent a good deal more time on his farm than he should have, and sometimes allowed his political enemies to gain control of national affairs while he managed the corn and potatoes. But even when he was where he belonged, he could not refrain from thinking how much better it was at home. When he arrived in Philadelphia for the first meeting of the Continental Congress, what struck him most forcefully was the superiority of Boston. "Philadelphia" he wrote in his diary, "with all its Trade, and Wealth, and Regularity is not Boston. The Morals of our People are much better, their Manners are more polite, and agreeable—they are purer English. Our language is better, our Persons are handsomer, our Spirit is greater, our Laws are wiser, our Religion is superior, our Education is better."[9] Later, when the Congress moved to Baltimore, he found that city even more deplorable, the dirtiest place in the world, and the inhabitants excessively haughty and greedy.[10] Wherever he went, whether Paris, London, or Amsterdam, it was the same story: no place was quite as good as Boston, and of course Boston was just a little inferior to Braintree.

Along with this provincialism went a bluntness of manner, a want of tact that made Adams less than ideally fitted to work with others in a legislative assembly. It was all he could do to sit through the tedious meanderings that always characterize debate in such bodies, and at the Continental Congress he was constantly annoyed when the other members failed to see at once the plain facts as he saw them. "In Congress, nibbling and quibbling—as usual," he would report to his diary. "There is no greater Mortification," he thought, "than to sit with half a dozen Witts, deliberating upon a Petition, Address, or Memorial. These great Witts, these subtle Criticks, these refined Genius's, these learned Lawyers, these wise Statesmen, are so fond of shewing their Parts and Powers, as to make their Consultations very tedious."[11] Later, as president of the United States, he sometimes found the members of his cabinet just as hard to bear. According to his friend Jefferson, Adams occasionally overcame opposition at cabinet meetings "by dashing and trampling his wig on the floor."[12]

Feebleness of mind in the cabinet officers he inherited from Washington may have driven Adams to this mode of expressing himself.[13] But his impatience extended to greater men too. He once had the audacity to find even Benjamin Franklin tedious. It was when he and Franklin shared a room together for the night at a tavern, and the two patriots argued about whether or not to open the window. Adams gave in and let Franklin open it, but then with characteristic ill grace he fell asleep while Franklin was explaining to him why fresh air was good for the health. And many years later when Franklin died at a ripe old age, Adams could not forbear recording that his final illness had been the result of a cold contracted while sleeping next to an open window.[14]

In an age noted for the versatility of its great men, Adams did not allow his keen mind much range. He once explained or rationalized his limitations by saying, "I must study Politicks and War that my sons may have liberty to study Mathematicks and Philosophy, Geography, natural History, Naval Architecture, navigation, Commerce and Agriculture, in order to give their Children a right to study Painting, Poetry, Musick, Architecture, Statuary, Tapestry, and Porcelaine."[15] But it seems unlikely that John Adams could have felt very comfortable with the fine arts, even if he could have been his own grandson.

His comments, for example, on art and architecture were painful. Landscape painting left him cold because he thought it was useless. After all, "The Sky, the Earth, Hills and Valleys, Rivers and Oceans, Forrests and Groves, Towns and Cities, may be seen at any time." The only important works of art, he thought, were those that taught morality. "The Story of the Prince, who lost his own Life in a bold attempt to save some of his subjects from a flood of Water"—this, he thought, was "worth all the Paintings that have been exhibited this Year."[16] He was equally naive in matters of science, and on one of the few occasions when he indulged in some brief scientific speculations about the nature of magnetism, he apologized to himself for wasting time on questions so entirely outside his sphere.[17] And anyone who reads these speculations will agree that the apology was due. Science was not Adams's métier.

Even in his chosen sphere of political thought his ideas were apt to be inflexible and doctrinaire. In his writings on the subject he hammered at the same point incessantly. He thought the solution to all problems of political organization was to be found in a bicameral legislature with a strong executive. This seemed to him to be the only lesson of history for politics, and he never tired of demonstrating it in volume after dreary volume, which he did not hesitate later to compare favorably with Locke, Harrington, Milton, Hume, and Montesquieu.[18]

There was never any false modesty in John Adams. Indeed, with all his other shortcomings went a palpable, potent, and pathetic vanity. John Adams was one of the vainest men who ever lived. He had an almost psychopathic yearning to be thought a great man by everybody. As a young man he frequently caught himself in the act of affecting great learning and wisdom in subjects that he actually knew little about, and like a good Puritan he chided himself for it in the pages of his diary.[19] But as he grew older he became much more expert at detecting vanity in others than in himself and displayed it so openly himself that sometimes he was the only one who failed to see it and earned the snickers of those around him.[20]

When he became one of the American commissioners to negotiate a peace treaty and joined Benjamin Franklin in Paris, he was beside himself with envy at the attention which the French showered on Franklin, and more than a little shocked by the freedom the ladies allowed the old man of kissing them "as often as he pleases."[21] He consoled himself by fishing for compliments from every Frenchman he met; and since the French were nothing if not polite, they furnished him with numerous little gems of praise which he confided lovingly to his diary: one obliging liar assured him that his French accent was much better than Franklin's; another told him that he was the George Washington of diplomacy. Adams beamed and recorded every detail in his diary.[22]

It is all rather poignant to read today, because in spite of his vanity, in spite of his provincialism, his narrowness, his tactlessness, John Adams was very nearly a great man. And his principal weakness, his vanity, was one of the sources of his greatness. For Adams's vanity was coupled with an ambition that enabled him to grow from a small-town lawyer-farmer into a world statesman.

There is a difference between vanity and ambition, a difference which Adams himself recognized. In his diary he never failed to chastise vanity whenever he recognized it, whether in himself or others; but from the outset he had a higher opinion of ambition and felt only scorn for persons who pursued their careers without a thought for fame. When he was only twenty-three he expressed his contempt for a physician who dabbled in trade instead of sticking hard at his practice. "These driveling souls, oh," exclaimed Adams, "He aims not at fame, only at a Living and a fortune."[23] At this time Adams himself was casting about for some quick and easy way to gratify his ambitions, some stroke that would catapult him instantly into renown. "Why have I not Genius," he asked himself, genius "to start some new Thought. Some thing that will surprize the World. New, grand, wild, yet regular Thought that may raise me at once to fame."[24] "Reputation," he told himself, "ought to be the perpetual subject of my Thoughts, and Aim of my Behaviour. How shall I gain a Reputation! How shall I Spread an Opinion of myself as a Lawyer of distinguished Genius, Learning, and Virtue?"[25] And as he tried to answer the question, every method seemed too long and tedious.

He was not the only young man who has dreamed of instant fame and success, and there have been some who never stopped looking for the bold stroke that would put them at the top. But as John Adams grew older, he also grew up. He gradually came to realize that the kind of success he wanted was not the kind to be won by some lucky stroke. Instant fame might be what his vanity craved, but his ambition reached for more enduring goals—and vanity in the end proved a weaker force than ambition. In the diary that he began to keep in 1755 at the age of twenty, one can watch his ambition overtake his vanity and harness it to ever larger purposes.

Keeping a diary was a New England habit, and in the diaries that New Englanders kept we can read the transformations of their civilization. The seventeenth-century writers used their diaries as account books in which to reckon up the daily signs of salvation or damnation they discerned in their souls. By John Adams's time, the doctrines of original sin and predestination had ceased to weigh heavily on young men of the Boston area, and the early pages of

Adams's diary are full of uncomplimentary references to clergy-men, full of free-thinking strictures on religious dogma and stereo-typed apostrophes to nature and nature's God. But if John Adams was not worried about original sin or the salvation of his soul, he substituted for the Puritan concern about these matters a concern about progress in his career. As his forebears had always found themselves lacking in devotion to God, Adams found himself lack-ing in devotion to his work and used the diary to urge himself to greater exertions. He found himself continually neglecting op-portunities for self-improvement. His span of attention was too short; he was always seeking diversions, daydreaming, going for long walks, or "gallanting the girls."[26] For long periods he ne-glected his diary, and upon resuming reproached himself for it.[27] Gradually he brought himself under control, stopped dreaming of lucky strokes, and became immersed in the pursuit of his calling, that of a lawyer. Though he continued to reproach himself for not working hard enough, the reproaches are about as convincing as those of Michael Wigglesworth, a Puritan minister who repeatedly chided himself for being the chief of sinners, that dubious dis-tinction which the most ardent seventeenth-century Puritans were always claiming for themselves.

John Adams not only learned to work hard, but he always worked for something more than money. Before he was admitted to the bar, Jeremy Gridley, the leading lawyer in Boston, advised him to "pursue the study of the Law rather than the Gain of it," and young Adams took the advice to heart.[28] He took the inter-esting cases rather than the lucrative ones and spent his time study-ing, studying, studying in the great English casebooks and the trea-tises written in Latin that he had to labor over sentence by sentence. The more he worked the more contemptuous he became of those whose goal was merely money or who sought or obtained success by some shortcut of the kind he had once longed for himself.

In these early years, before the contest with England began, John Adams reminds one of an earlier New England diarist, John Winthrop, who also had a hard time as a young man in driving himself to work but gradually gained self-control and won the respect of his neighbors as a man who took a large view of things. There are other resemblances too. Both men originally considered entering the ministry but turned to law. Both men loved New England, served her well, and resented efforts by England to control her. Both were sensitive to criticism, suspected the worst of their opponents, and felt obliged constantly to offer lengthy defenses of their conduct to the world and to themselves. Both thought that the good life lay in hard work at one's calling, whatever that calling might be. But most importantly, both men were summoned by the events of their time to a much larger role in the world than they could have expected. If it had not been for the founding of Massachusetts, John Winthrop would have been a country squire and part-time lawyer. Instead he was the first great statesman of a Puritan commonwealth in a new world. If it had not been for the American Revolution, John Adams would have been a learned lawyer and part-time farmer, but his reputation would scarcely have reached beyond Braintree and Boston. Instead he became one of the architects of American independence and one of the first great statesmen of a new nation.

There were other Americans of this period, Franklin for example, and perhaps Jefferson, who would have attained a large stature in any century or any country. But John Adams was not born great nor would he in all probability have achieved greatness by his own efforts in the British Empire as it was constituted when he was born. It was one of the weaknesses of the empire that it offered no arena larger than that of provincial politics for the political talents of its colonial subjects. Adams was one of those whom the patriot historian David Ramsay had in mind when Ramsay looked back in 1789 on the events of the preceding twenty-five years and observed that the American Revolution "gave occasion for the display of abilities which, but for that event, would have been lost to the world," that the Revolution seemed not only to require but to create talents. "Men whose minds were warmed with the love of liberty, and whose abilities were improved by daily exercise, and sharpened with a laudable ambition to serve their distressed country, spoke, wrote, and acted, with an energy far surpassing all expectations which could be reasonably founded on their previous acquirements."[29]

In the case of John Adams, the laudable ambition that Ramsay described made its appearance at the time of the Stamp Act, when the young lawyer who pursued the study rather than the gain of the law concluded at once that the Stamp Act was illegal and unconstitutional, an attempt to impose on Americans the tyrannical system which their forefathers had fled to the wilderness in order to escape. When the Massachusetts judges closed their courts because they lacked stamped paper on which to conduct business, Adams was one of those who called upon them to open their doors and ignore the Stamp Act. In his view it was the duty of the courts to pronounce such an unconstitutional act null and void and to proceed to business as though it had never been passed.[30]

Characteristically he worried over the enforced idleness that was thrust upon him by the closing of the courts. He resolved to redeem the time in more study, and he wrote articles for the newspapers to demonstrate the injustice and unconstitutionality of the act.[31] But Adams's discontent with the Stamp Act was not simply the product of his study of law. Parliament's attempt to tax the colonies, to take away the property of men without their consent, struck at one of his deepest feelings, a feeling that he shared with many other Americans. For a threat to property was a threat to his beloved farm. Adams knew something at first hand of what it meant to turn forested wilderness into pasture and plowland. His feeling for his land at Braintree, which helped to make him always a provincial, also gave him something in common with the hundreds of thousands of ordinary men in America who spent their days on the land and who derived from their work with ax and plow that special feeling for property peculiar to Americans, who believed that work was an essential ingredient of property. John Adams was dedicated to hard work, whether at his law office or on his land, and in his passionate response to British taxation he gave expression to feelings that were as common in Charleston, South Carolina, or Lancaster, Pennsylvania, as they were in Braintree, Massachusetts.

In the years that followed, as the customs commissioners arrived in Boston and began their racketeering activities, and as the British government awarded soft jobs to its favorites, Adams's dedication to work was more and more affronted by the sight of men who had discovered a political shortcut to success and wealth. There was nothing more obnoxious to him than the man who satisfied his ambition and avarice by obtaining appointments from the crown. In Massachusetts the man who had gained most success in this way was the lieutenant governor, Thomas Hutchinson, and Adams never tired of denouncing Hutchinson. "Has he not grasped four of the most important offices in the Province into his own Hands?" asked Adams. "Has not his Brother in Law Oliver another of the greatest Places in Government? Is not a Brother of the Secretary, a Judge of the Superior Court? Has not that Brother a son in the House? Has not the secretary a son in the House, who is also a Judge in one of the Counties? Did not that son marry the Daughter of another of the Judges of the Superior Court? Has not the Lieutenant Governor a Brother, a Judge of the Pleas in Boston? And a Namesake and near Relation who is another Judge? Has not the Lieutenant Governor a near Relation who is Register of his own Court of Probate, and Deputy Secretary? Has he not another near Relation who is Clerk of the House of Representatives? Is not this amazing ascendancy of one Family, Foundation sufficient on which to erect a Tyranny? Is it not enough to excite Jealousies among the People?"[32]

It was enough certainly to excite alarm and perhaps a little jealousy in John Adams, who viewed such office-mongering not only as wicked but as un-American. For already by 1765 Adams was beginning to identify virtue with America and vice with England. Adams retained throughout his life an almost unbounded admiration for the special English achievement in government: the distribution of authority among king, Lords, and Commons. It was the separation of powers among these distinct bodies that had enabled England to become the bearer of freedom to the modern world. But freedom was always the child of virtue, and vice had found a way to sap the strength of English freedom. Through places, pensions, and sinecures the king and his ministers had invaded the legislative branch and built a network of sycophantic supporters in both Lords and Commons. By finding lucrative positions for friends and relatives who showed the right subservience, they had enabled the executive to dominate the legislature. English freedom, if still alive, was fast succumbing to corruption. And the cancer could spread to America through the avarice of men like Hutchinson, with his web of fawning relatives, all bent on a political shortcut to wealth and power.[38]

Adams was sure that America could resist the evil if men like himself stood out against the insidious process. England had carried freedom into the modern world but was failing to cherish it. Now in this dark hour it was up to Americans to keep freedom alive in the world. Americans, Adams wrote in a piece intended for the newspapers, were predestined for this special role. "They know," he said, "that Liberty has been skulking about in Corners from the Creation, and has been hunted and persecuted, in all Countries, by cruel Power. But they flatter themselves that America was designed by Providence for the Theatre, on which Man was to make his true figure, on which science, Virtue, Liberty, Happiness and Glory were to exist in Peace."[34]

If the words had a pompous ring to them, they nevertheless struck a chord that was beginning to sound throughout the colonies. In their resistance to Parliament, Americans saw themselves as conservatives in the best sense of the word. Their task was conservation, the conservation of freedom, and in the New World freedom might bring to its devotees such rewards as could scarcely be dreamt of in an Old World grown accustomed to tyranny and corruption.

Adams had not yet considered what was to be his own precise role in the conservation of freedom. He continued throughout the

1760s and 1770s to practice law and declined to be drawn into the web of royal appointments that might have gratified his vanity and opened a road to greater wealth. His outspoken hostility to Parliamentary policy and to the men who carried it out made him a popular figure in Boston, and he already took a larger view of the struggle than most of his fellow townsmen. After the Boston Massacre, when other Boston lawyers hesitated to undertake the defense of the British soldiers who had fired on the crowd before the customhouse, Adams reluctantly but resolutely agreed to do it. No man in a free country, he felt, should be denied the right to counsel, and furthermore a proper defense of the soldiers would alert the people of America to the danger in which they stood when soldiers were quartered among them. Events of this kind were to be expected when government abdicated its functions to the military. It was not the soldiers who were at fault but the British government. Adams not only defended the soldiers but secured an acquittal.[35]

He did not, however, at any moment become less hostile to the policies of Great Britain. In the years from 1770 to 1773, when relations with the mother country were temporarily improved and Governor Hutchinson was enjoying a newfound popularity, Adams continued to be suspicious and bitter. He surprised even himself by the violence of his feelings when an English gentleman visiting Boston struck up a conversation with him about a royal commission that was investigating the burning of a naval vessel (the *Gaspée*) by a Rhode Island mob. "I found," he confessed to his diary, that "the old Warmth, Heat, Violence, Acrimony, Bitterness, Sharpness of my Temper, and Expression, was not departed. I said there was no more Justice left in Britain than there was in Hell— That I wished for War, and that the whole Bourbon Family was upon the Back of Great Britain—avowed a thorough Disaffection to that Country—wished that any Thing might happen to them, and that as the Clergy prayed of our Enemies in Time of War, they might be brought to reason or to ruin." Afterwards he was ashamed of this outburst and berated himself for not having better control of his tongue, but there was no doubt about the way he felt.[36]

There is, I think, an explanation for the fact that Adams continued to feel so passionately bitter against Great Britain at a time when the feelings of many other colonists were softening. In the opposition to the Stamp Act and to the royal placeholders and to the continuing Parliamentary efforts to tax the Americans, Adams had begun to sense, perhaps not quite consciously, that a new field of activity was opening for Americans like himself, for men of large ambition, men who loved the land and were dedicated to hard work, but who wished to work for something more than money and for a larger success than that of a local lawyer. Adams scorned the wider field of operations that would have been open to him if he had accepted office under the crown,[37] and even in the royal service an American could aspire to no significant office that would extend in its jurisdiction beyond a single colony. But in fighting British taxation Americans in every colony had begun to act together and to think in terms of the whole continent. Before 1774 there were no institutions in which this way of thought could find an outlet in action. But with the meeting of the first Continental Congress an institution of continental scope came into existence, and Adams, attending it, found at last a field of action commensurate with his ambition.

At the time when the first Congress met, Adams may already have reached the position where he was prepared for Massachusetts to set up a popular government of its own in defiance of royal authority.[38] But he knew that it was imperative for the rest of the colonies to go along with Massachusetts, to make resistance to Britain an American cause, not a New England one. To this end he was willing to listen endlessly to the speeches that rambled from the point, to the wits who felt obliged to show their sophistication, and even to the cautious conservatives who wanted to avoid giving offense of any kind to the mother country. The very existence of a continental congress was exciting to Adams, and participation in it constantly expanded his ambitions for America—and for himself. Long before most of the other delegates were ready to think of independence, John Adams had his heart set on it, independence not merely for Massachusetts but for the continent.[39] And when others began to wonder whether the colonies should move toward independence, Adams was already thinking about ways to achieve and maintain it. Indeed the achievement and preservation of American independence became inseparable from his own ambition. One can understand his subsequent role in American history only by bearing in mind how closely Adams identified himself with the independence of the United States.

At the Continental Congress, although he possessed outstanding literary gifts, he was not outstanding in the drafting of documents for public consumption. His most significant contribution in this respect was in phrasing a resolution about Parliament's authority with sufficient ambiguity to satisfy both radicals and moderates.[40] Though he was later on the committee that drafted the Declaration of Independence, he contributed little to it. It was not a declaration of independence that he wanted so much as the fact of independence, and he concentrated on maneuvering the Congress to prepare for the actual independence that he was sure they would come to in the end.[41]

No man in Congress had a clearer idea of what independence would entail: the risks, obligations, and burdens that it would impose on Americans. Adams welcomed the burdens; and in Congress he nudged the other delegates, step by step, to pick them up, until they were in fact already acting as an independent nation, before their declaration proclaimed that status.

After the Battle of Lexington he persuaded them to enlist the Continental Army under the command of George Washington. Adams threw his weight toward the selection of the Virginian instead of the Yankee contender for the post, John Hancock, in order to keep the war and the army an American rather than a New England affair.[42] Adams was even more concerned to furnish the fighting colonies with a navy than with an army. Long before they declared independence Adams had seen that their ultimate independence of action as a nation would depend on an ability to protect their own commerce on the high seas. Adams, though without previous experience in international politics, recognized at once the crucial importance of sea power and throughout his career was an ardent if not always successful advocate of a strong United States Navy.[43]

After the Congress did declare independence, Adams continued to serve in the exciting new arena of national politics; and when he retired for a time to mend his private affairs, his colleagues challenged him with a larger assignment by offering him successive missions to Europe, first to represent the United States (along with Benjamin Franklin and Arthur Lee) at the French court and then as one of the commissioners (along with Franklin and John Jay) to negotiate peace with England. In both roles Adams was so zealously protective of American independence, so suspicious in sensing threats to it, that both European diplomats and his fellow commissioners sometimes found him a prickly character to deal with. Thomas Jefferson, who knew him from their days together in Congress, was uneasy when he heard of Adams's appointment to the peace commission. "He hates Franklin," Jefferson mused, "he hates Jay, he hates the French, he hates the English. To whom will he adhere?"[44] The answer was easy enough. Adams adhered to the United States and made life difficult for anyone whose attachment to the nation seemed to him less zealous than his own. The French, in particular, thought him difficult. And doubtless he was.[45]

Before he ever set foot in France he had been dubious about the French alliance that Congress was negotiating (it was signed by the time he arrived), and he was troubled by the military aid that resulted from it. Americans, he felt, ought to fight their own battles, build their own navy, raise their own armies. They should accept only economic, commercial assistance from France. To win independence with the help of another country seemed to Adams to be degrading, to show a lack of the virtue which had hitherto characterized his countrymen in their struggle against England and which he embraced as the proudest attribute of the new nation he wanted to build.[46]

When he arrived in France, he discovered another reason for

keeping the United States as free as possible from all connection with that country and the rest of Europe. In the struggle with England, Adams had come to identify the mother country with vice and corruption, prodigality and laziness, frivolity and luxury, the classical characteristics of a degenerate monarchy. America, on the other hand, he identified with virtue, simple living, frugality, and hard work, the classical characteristics of a republic. In France he saw that America's new ally was no better than her enemy, indeed much worse. He got his first lesson when his ship landed at Bordeaux and he was invited to a dinner party. There he found to his surprise that French ladies did not sit next to their husbands. One bold and attractive young woman, placed next to him, opened the conversation with typical French wit by saying: "Mr. Adams, by your Name I conclude you are descended from the first Man and Woman, and probably in your family may be preserved the tradition which may resolve a difficulty which I could never explain. I never could understand how the first Couple found out the Art of lying together." The Braintree farmer, the Boston lawyer, the new American statesman was shocked, but if John Adams remained a provincial, he was never speechless. "I thought it would be as well," he decided, "to set a brazen face against a brazen face and answer a fool according to her folly." Accordingly he assumed a grave air and answered: "Madame my Family resembles the first Couple both in the name and in their frailties so much that I have no doubt We are descended from that in Paradise. But the subject is perfectly understood by Us, whether by tradition I can not tell: I rather think it is by Instinct, for there is a Physical quality in Us resembling the Power of Electricity or of the Magnet, by which when a Pair approach within a striking distance they fly together like the Needle to the Pole or like two Objects in electric Experiments." Adams thought of adding "in a lawful way" after "within a striking distance" but decided that the lady would only have thought it an example of provincial pedantry or bigotry. But she had the last word anyhow, for she replied to his electric explanation by saying, "Well I know not how it was, but this I know, it is a very happy shock." All of which left Adams with the reflection that "if such are the manners of Women of Rank, Fashion and Reputation in France, they can never support a Republican Government nor be reconciled with it. We must therefore take great care not to import them into America." Adams's provincialism refined by republicanism had become triumphant nationalism.[47]

The union of nationalism and republicanism in Adams's mind was, for the moment at least, complete. There was no doubt that the new American nation must have a republican government; and he was sure that even in a world full of monarchies an American republic could succeed—at least as long as the country remained attached to sound morality and hard work. Nothing that he saw in either France or England made him think that those countries could ever support the free republican institutions that were possible among the virtuous Americans. And everything that he saw increased his conviction that the ability of the American republic to sustain its independence rested on the ability of its citizens to sustain their virtue. Any assistance they received from Europe would be contaminated. "America will never derive any good from Europe of any Kind," was his conclusion after two years in France and Holland. "I wish," he wrote to his uncle, Cotton Tufts, "We were wise enough to depend upon ourselves for every thing and upon them for nothing."[48]

Unfortunately his countrymen were not that wise. In his absence the Congress so completely succumbed to the blandishments of the French ambassador, La Luzerne, that it sent instructions to the peace commissioners to be guided by the French court in all their negotiations. Adams was horrified at this groveling subservience and joined the other commissioners in ignoring the instructions. He perceived, when British pride prevented the British from doing so, that it would be to the advantage of Britain in the European balance of power to court the favor of the independent United States.[49] And he also perceived, when sentiment and gratitude prevented Americans from seeing it, that once the war was over, it would no longer be to the advantage of France to extend favors to America or assist its growth in power.[50] Accordingly, though he hated the British as cordially as ever, he tried to establish friendly relations with England and to avoid committing the United States too heavily to France. He wanted the United States to preserve its freedom of action. What he feared most was that the French and British would draw the United States into the maelstrom of European politics by fostering pro-French and pro-British political factions or parties in America.[51] The fear proved to be well founded.

Such parties did arise in the United States in the 1790s. Adams found himself at that time both president of the United States and the head of the party that was pro-English. But Adams himself had never been pro anything except the United States, and he gave the final measure of his own deep attachment to the country's independence when he led it away from war with France. During his administration popular feeling against France ran high. The French seized American ships on the high seas and insulted our representatives abroad. Congress authorized a navy, a standing army, and extra provisional forces to deal with the situation. If Adams had said the word, war would have come.[52]

Adams refused to say it, not because he had become less concerned about American vulnerability to foreign aggression, not because his attitude toward the French had softened. His opinion of them had in fact sunk steadily with the passing years, and for a time he had been persuaded that war was the safest response to the danger they posed. But in spite of his own belligerence and in spite of the insults and seizures the United States had suffered, Adams's final judgment of the crisis was that the protection of American independence did not dictate war. The economic strain of a war, while the Revolutionary War debt was still unpaid, might weaken the ability of the nation to withstand later threats of aggression. Or it might force the United States to seek shelter under the guns of the British navy and thereby turn the country (as his son would put it twenty-four years later) into a cockboat in the wake of the British man-of-war. It could also exacerbate the factional divisions that were already troubling the republic, and Adams was well aware that a republic could be shattered as effectively by internal strife as by foreign aggression. Ever since the formation of the American Union the European powers had been expecting it to fall apart and were waiting to pick up the pieces. They would not have the chance if John Adams could help it.[53]

The battle for American independence had been for Adams a kind of regeneration, an almost religious experience, which transformed his life. He had spent his years in the Continental Congress striving to keep Americans pulling together toward independence. After independence was won he had spent the years guarding it and broadening his grasp of what was and was not crucial to it. War in the year 1799, he decided, was not crucial. Consequently, in the face of demands for a larger army and war with France, John Adams called for a smaller army, a larger navy, and no war. To top it off, he sent a peace mission to France. By so doing he wrecked his career as a politician, for he split his party, and the other leaders of it never forgave him.[54]

But Adams, for all his vanity, had grown to value the approval of a political party at no higher rate than the acclaim of a dinner party. What he valued most was American independence and the virtue that must sustain it—not least his own. In ending his political career he crushed his vanity but satisfied his ambition. And he was rightly proud of the gesture throughout the remainder of his life. He may or may not have been a great man. But he had shown that he was a great American.

NOTES

1. E. G. R. Taylor, ed., *The Original Writings and Correspondence of the Two Richard Hakluyts*, Works issued by the Hakluyt Society, 2d ser., 76, 77 (London, 1935), 1:142–43.

2. J. M. Bumsted, "'Things in the Womb of Time': Ideas of American Independence, 1663 to 1763," *William and Mary Quarterly*, 3d ser., 31 (1974): 533–64.

3. E. S. Morgan, ed., *Prologue to Revolution: Sources and Documents on the Stamp Act Crisis, 1764–1766* (Chapel Hill, N.C., 1959), p. 62; Worthington C. Ford

et al., eds., *Journals of the Continental Congress, 1774–1789* (Washington, D.C., 1904–37), 1:115–21, 2:155; Thomas Jefferson, *The Papers of Thomas Jefferson,* ed. Julian P. Boyd (Princeton, N.J., 1950–), 1:187–219.

4. S. E. Morison, ed., *Sources and Documents Illustrating the American Revolution, 1764–1788* (Oxford, 1923), pp. 186–203; *Journals of the Continental Congress,* 11:585, 605–15.

5. L. H. Butterfield et al., eds., *Diary and Autobiography of John Adams* (Cambridge, Mass., 1961), 2:54–55.

6. Bernard Bailyn, *The Ordeal of Thomas Hutchinson* (Cambridge, Mass., 1974), p. 276. Even when John Adams arrived in France in 1778 as U.S. commissioner, the French supposed he must be the "famous" Mr. Adams, and it was a matter of some mortification to him to point out that he was not (*Diary and Autobiography,* 2:351).

7. The most valuable recent discussion of the role of Galloway in the Congress is in David Ammerman, *In the Common Cause: American Response to the Coercive Acts* (Charlottesville, Va., 1974), esp. pp. 58–60, 89–101. The standard biography of Samuel Adams is John C. Miller, *Sam Adams: Pioneer in Propaganda* (Boston, 1936); the standard biography of John Adams is Page Smith, *John Adams* (New York, 1962).

8. *Diary and Autobiography,* 3:193–94.

9. Ibid., 2:150.

10. Ibid., 2:258, 260.

11. Ibid., 2:156.

12. Thomas Jefferson, *The Writings of Thomas Jefferson,* ed. Paul Leicester Ford (New York and London, 1892–99), 9:70.

13. Adams was persuaded that Washington had left office after two terms because he could not persuade abler men to join the cabinet: "He was driven to the Necessity of appointing such as would accept. And this necessity was, in my Opinion the real cause of his retirement from office: for you may depend upon it, that retirement was not voluntary" (to Thomas Jefferson, July 3, 1813, L. J. Cappon, ed., *The Adams-Jefferson Letters: The Complete Correspondence between Thomas Jefferson and Abigail and John Adams* [Chapel Hill, N.C., 1959], 2:349).

14. *Diary and Autobiography,* 3:418–19.

15. To Abigail Adams, May 1780, L. H. Butterfield et al., eds., *Adams Family Correspondence* (Cambridge, Mass., 1963–), 3:342.

16. *Diary and Autobiography,* 3:192.

17. Ibid., 3:136, 137n.

18. To Thomas Jefferson, July 15, 1813, *Adams-Jefferson Letters,* 2:357. The volumes referred to are those comprising *A Defence of the Constitutions of the United States* (London, 1787–88) and *Discourses on Davila* (Boston, 1805)

reprinted in *Works*, ed. Charles Francis Adams (Boston, 1850–56), vols. 4–6. Adams also embodied his views in extensive marginal notations in the books of his library, which have been skillfully edited in the form of a dialogue between Adams and the authors in Zoltan Haraszti, *John Adams and the Prophets of Progress* (Cambridge, Mass., 1952). The best discussion of Adams's political ideas is John R. Howe, Jr., *The Changing Political Thought of John Adams* (Princeton, N.J., 1966).

19. *Diary and Autobiography*, 1:37, 68, 106.

20. When he heard the snickers or echoes of them, he was sufficiently candid with himself to admit that he had a measure of vanity. In a letter that he drafted (but apparently did not send) to Elbridge Gerry (May 2, 1785, Adams Papers microfilm, reel 364) he acknowledged the weakness but could not refrain from suggesting that Washington and Franklin had more of it and that indeed all great men suffered from it whether they admitted it or not. Cf. *Diary and Autobiography*, 3:177n. For some other observations of Adams on his own vanity, see his letters to Benjamin Rush, April 22, 1782, and July 23, 1806, in Alexander Biddle, *Old Family Letters Copied from the Originals*, ser. A (Philadelphia, 1892), pp. 21, 106–7.

21. To Abigail Adams, April 25, 1778, *Family Correspondence*, 3:17.

22. *Diary and Autobiography*, 2:389, 3:50; cf. 2:302.

23. Ibid., 1:53.

24. Ibid., 1:95.

25. Ibid., 1:78.

26. Ibid., 1:57, 72–73, 86, 87, 118, 127, 131–33, 168, 173–74, 200, 218, 229–30.

27. Ibid., 1:263, 2:52, 67.

28. Ibid., 1:55, 3:272.

29. David Ramsay, *The History of the American Revolution* (Philadelphia, 1789), 2:315–16.

30. *Diary and Autobiography*, 1:263–64, 267–70.

31. *Boston Gazette*, Jan. 13, 20, 27, 1766; *Diary and Autobiography*, 1:264, 272, 274–77, 281–82, 287–92, 296–99.

32. *Diary and Autobiography*, 1:260. Cf. ibid., 1:281, 305–6, 310–11, 2:34–35, 39, 42–43.

33. Ibid., 1:277, 280; *Family Correspondence*, 1:116–17, 124–25.

34. *Diary and Autobiography*, 1:282.

35. Ibid., 2:74, 79, 84, 3:292–96. All were acquitted of murder, but two were convicted of manslaughter.

36. Ibid., 2:76.

37. But Adams's recollection of his refusal of one offer of office differed from that of those who made the offer (ibid., 3:286–89).

38. See, for example, his letter to Abigail, July 6, 1774, *Family Correspondence*,

1:126–28, and his later recollections, in letters to Benjamin Rush, that he had been thinking about independence since 1755 and that he considered the non-importation, nonexportation agreements adopted by the first Congress as so much labor lost, since he was already convinced that war was inevitable (Biddle, *Old Family Letters,* pp. 134–41, 207 [May 1, 21, 1807, Oct. 10, 1808]).

39. To James Warren, July 6, 1775, *Warren-Adams Letters: Being Chiefly a Correspondence among John Adams, Samuel Adams, and James Warren,* Massachusetts Historical Society, *Collections,* 72, 73 (1917, 1925), 1:73–75; to Abigail Adams, July 3, 1776, *Family Correspondence,* 2:29–33.

40. *Diary and Autobiography,* 3:309–10. Adams's recollection of his contribution was somewhat larger than the contemporary evidence will support. See Edmund C. Burnett, *The Continental Congress* (New York, 1941), pp. 52–54.

41. *Diary and Autobiography,* 2:231, 3:327–30. See also his letter to Abigail, April 14, 1776, *Family Correspondence,* 1:382: "As to Declarations of Independency, be patient. Read our Privateering Laws, and our Commercial Laws. What signifies a Word." It is not without significance, in spite of this disparagement of the mere word "Independency," that Adams uses the pregnant word "Laws" to describe congressional actions.

42. *Diary and Autobiography,* 3:321–24; *Family Correspondence,* 1:215–16.

43. To James Warren, Oct. 19, 1775, *Warren-Adams Letters,* 1:145–46; to Benjamin Rush, Sept. 20, 1780, Biddle, *Old Family Letters,* p. 20; *Diary and Autobiography,* 2:145, 198, 201–2n (and references cited there), 3:328, 342–51, 377, 4:198.

44. Jefferson, *Papers,* 6:241 (to James Madison, Feb. 14, 1783). Jefferson himself was appointed a member of the commission but was unable to attend.

45. The standard account of the negotiations is Richard B. Morris, *The Peacemakers: The Great Powers and American Independence* (New York, 1965).

46. *Diary and Autobiography,* 3:328–29, 337–38; to James Warren, Oct. 7, 1775, May 3, 1777, *Warren-Adams Letters,* 1:126–29, 322; to John Winthrop, June 23, 1776, Edmund C. Burnett, ed., *Letters of Members of the Continental Congress* (Washington, D.C., 1921–38), 1:502; to Benjamin Rush, Sept. 30, 1805, Biddle, *Old Family Letters,* pp. 79–82. Adams claimed that Washington and Jefferson derived from him their policy of no entangling alliances (ibid., p. 71 [to Benjamin Rush, July 7, 1805]).

47. *Diary and Autobiography,* 4:36–37. I have corrected the tenses to make them all present. Adams began in the present tense, shifted to the past, and then shifted back to the present. Adams continued to think that republican government depended heavily on feminine virtue. In 1807 he wrote to Benjamin Rush that "national Morality never was and never can be preserved, without the utmost purity and chastity in women: and without national Morality a Republican Government cannot be maintained. Therefore my dear Fellow

Citizens of America, you must ask leave of your wives and daughters to pre-serve your Republick" (Biddle, *Old Family Letters,* p. 128).

48. Dec. 9, 1780, *Family Correspondence,* 4:29.

49. *Diary and Autobiography,* 3:63–64, 91–92.

50. Ibid., 3:92–93, 115–16, 121–22.

51. Ibid., 3:51–52, 328–29.

52. Alexander DeConde, *The Quasi-War: The Politics and Diplomacy of the Un-declared War with France, 1797–1801* (New York, 1966).

53. Stephen G. Kurtz, *The Presidency of John Adams* (Philadelphia, 1957); Kurtz, "The French Mission of 1799–1800: Concluding Chapter in the Statecraft of John Adams," *Political Science Quarterly* 80 (1965):543–57.

54. In later life Adams may have exaggerated both the significance of his deci-sion and the opposition to it by his cabinet, but there can be no doubt that the decision was his and that it alienated other Federalists. See Jacob E. Cooke, "Country above Party: John Adams and the 1799 Mission to France," in Ed-mund P. Willis, ed., *Fame and the Founding Fathers* (Bethlehem, Pa., 1967), pp. 53–77.

~ 2 ~

GEORGE WASHINGTON

THE KING OF ENGLAND, GEORGE III, WAS FOND OF FARMING. His favorite diversion was to ride about his lands, chatting with the tenants about the crops. "Farmer George," he called himself. His arch-opponent, George Washington, had the same fondness for farming. He too enjoyed riding about his lands and talking about the crops. Indeed there was nothing else he enjoyed quite so much. But there the likeness ceased. And among the many other matters that differentiated George Washington from George III, none was more striking than his greater dignity and reserve. George Washington would never have taken the liberty of calling himself "Farmer George," nor would he have allowed anyone else to do so. Even his close friends took care to keep their distance, and those who forgot to were apt to be brought up sharp.

A familiar anecdote, though perhaps apocryphal, well illustrates Washington's customary posture toward himself and toward others. During the meeting of the Constitutional Convention in Philadelphia in 1787 a group of Washington's friends were remarking on his extraordinarily reserved and remote manner, even among his most intimate acquaintances. Gouverneur Morris, who was always full of boldness and wit, had the nerve to disagree. He could be as familiar with Washington, he said, as with any of his other friends. Alexander Hamilton called his bluff by offering to provide a supper and wine for a dozen of them if Morris would, at the next reception Washington gave, simply walk up to him, gently slap him on the shoulder, and say, "My dear General, how happy I am to see you look so well." On the appointed evening a substantial number were already present when Morris arrived, walked up to Washington, bowed, shook hands, and then placed his left hand on Washington's shoulder and said, "My dear General, I am very happy to see you look so well." The response was immediate and icy. Washington reached up and removed the hand, stepped back, and fixed his eye in silence on Morris, until Morris retreated abashed into the crowd. The company looked on in embarrassment, and no one ever tried it again.[1]

It seems a most un-American reaction, not the sort of thing that Americans like to see in the men they honor, certainly not the sort of thing one would look for in the leader of a popular revolution today. Yet Americans then and since have honored George Washington far beyond any other man in their history. Moreover, he earned the honor, and his dignity and reserve, the aloofness that still separates him from us, helped him to earn it.

How this came about is part of the larger story of American independence, the story of how the American Revolution transformed some of the least lovable traits of a seemingly ordinary man into national assets. For besides his aloofness, Washington had other characteristics which at this distance appear less than admirable, but which served him and the nation well in the struggle for independence.

Perhaps the most conspicuous of these traits, conspicuous at least in his surviving correspondence, was an unabashed concern for his own economic interest. Although Washington was fair in his dealings and did not ask favor of any man, he kept a constant, wary, and often cold eye on making a profit, ever suspicious (and not always without reason) that other men were trying to take advantage of him. Like most Virginia planters he complained that London merchants were giving him too little for his tobacco or charging him too much for the goods he bought from them.[2] When he rented to tenants, he demanded to be paid punctually and dismissed men's inability to meet their obligations as irresponsibility or knavery.[3] If a man was so foolish as to try cheating him, he was capable of a fury that comes through vividly in his letters, as when he wrote to one associate that "all my concern is that I ever engag'd myself in behalf of so ungrateful and dirty a fellow as you are."[4]

In operating his plantation at Mount Vernon he inveighed endlessly against waste of time, waste of supplies, waste of money. "A penny saved is a penny got," he would say, or "Many mickles make a muckle," by which he apparently meant that many small savings would add up to a large one.[5] Even in dealings with his mother he was watchful, for he thought she had extravagant tastes. He was ready to supply her real wants, he said, but found her "*imaginary wants . . . indefinite and oftentimes insatiable.*"[6]

Even after he left Mount Vernon in order to win a war and found a nation, his intense absorption with his estate persisted, somehow curiously out of place now, and out of proportion to the historic events that he was grappling with. In the darkest hours of the war and later during some of the tensest national crises he took time to write to the managers of his plantation about making it show a profit. In early December 1776, for example, after fleeing across the Delaware with the remnants of his army, he sent home instructions to make do without buying linen for the slaves "as the price is too heavy to be borne with."[7] And while he was president, his weekly directives to his managers far exceeded in length the documents he prepared for his subordinates in government.

No detail was too small for his attention. In December 1792, while his cabinet was rent by the feud between Jefferson and Hamilton, he sent orders that Anthony's sore toe "should be examined and if it requires it something should be done to it, otherwise, as usual, it will serve him as a pretence to be in the house half the Winter."[8] Three months later, when Hamilton was under attack in the House of Representatives for alleged corruption in the Treasury Department, Washington was worried that Caroline, "who was never celebrated for her honesty," would steal some of the linen she had been entrusted with cutting.[9] And shortly thereafter when war broke out in Europe and the cabinet was debating what attitude the United States should take toward the belligerents, the president professed himself to be "extremely anxious," because he wanted some honey locust seed to be planted before it was too late, and he wanted his sheep to be washed before they were sheared. "Otherwise," he feared, "I shall have a larger part of the Wool stolen if washed after it is sheared."[10]

As the quotations suggest, Washington was continually alert against theft, embezzlement, and shirking by his slaves. Slaves would not work, he warned his managers and overseers again and again, unless they were continually watched. And they would take every opportunity to steal. They would feign sickness to avoid work. They would stay up all night enjoying themselves and be too tired the next day to get anything done. They would use every pretext to take advantage of him, like Peter, who was charged with riding about the plantation to look after the stock but, Washington suspected, was usually "in pursuit of other objects; either of traffic or amusement, more advancive of his own pleasures than my benefit."[11]

Washington's opinion of his managers and overseers was hardly better. He hired a succession of them who never seemed able to satisfy him. In 1793, after a bad year, he got off a series of blistering letters to the overseers of the five farms into which Mount Vernon was divided. Hyland Crow, for example, was guilty of "insufferable neglect" in failing to get fields plowed before frost. "And look ye, Mr. Crow," wrote the president, "I have too good reasons to believe that your running about, and entertaining company at home . . . is the cause of this, now, irremediable evil in the progress of my business." And Thomas Green, in charge of the plantation's carpenters, got a similar tongue-lashing. "I know full well," said Washington, "that to speak to you is of no more avail, than to speak to a bird that is flying over one's head; first, because you are lost to all sense of shame, and to every feeling that ought to govern an honest man, who sets any store by his character; and secondly, because you have no more command of the people over whom you are placed, than I have over the beasts of the forists: for if they chuse to work they may; if they do not you have not influence enough to make them."[12]

And so it went. No one ever worked hard enough at Mount Vernon, and when the owner was there, he felt obliged to ride daily around the place (or so he told himself) in order to keep people at their jobs and to point out to his manager what was not being done right. When a manager took offense at the constant criticism, Washington assured him "that I shall never relinquish the right of judging, in my own concerns. . . . If I cannot remark upon my own business, passing every day under my eyes, without hurting your feelings, I must discontinue my rides, or become a cypher on my own Estate."[13]

A cipher Washington would not be and could not be. He would run his own affairs in his own interest. And he was very good at it. But if that was all he had done, we should never have heard of him, except perhaps as one of many prosperous Virginia planters. Fortunately it was not merely interest that moved him. Dearer by far to him was honor. Honor required a man to be assiduous and responsible in looking after his interests. But honor also required a man to look beyond his own profit, though where he looked and how far might be a question that different men would answer differently.

At the simplest, most superficial level Washington's love of honor showed itself in a concern with outward appearances. His attachment to Mount Vernon, for example, did not stop at the desire to make a profit from it. He wanted the place and its surroundings to look right, to honor the owner by the way they looked; and this meant giving up the slovenly, though often profitable, agricultural practices of his neighbors. He stopped growing tobacco and turned to the rotation of cereal crops that were approved by the English agricultural reformers of the time. He tried, mostly in vain, to substitute handsome English hedgerows for the crude rail fences of Virginia. And he insisted that all weeds and brush be grubbed out of his plowed fields, not simply for the sake of productivity, but because the fields looked better that way. He would rather, he said, have one acre properly cleansed than five prepared in the usual way.[14]

Similarly, as commander in chief, he wanted his soldiers to look right. Their uniforms must be kept in order and "well put on." Otherwise, he said, there would be "little difference in *appearance* between a soldier in rags and a Soldier in uniform."[15] Appearance mattered especially to him when French troops were coming; his army must not be dishonored by looking shabby or careless. Even the huts for winter quarters must be built of an identical size: "any hut not exactly conformable to the plan, or the least out of line, shall be pulled down and built again agreeable to the model and in it's proper place."[16] And when Washington became president, he showed the same concern for appearances in furnishing his house and decorating his coach in a plain but elegant style that he thought was appropriate for the head of a republican government.[17]

But a man who craved honor could not gain it simply by putting up a good appearance. This was only a shade removed from vanity, and Washington from the beginning betrayed none of the vanity of a John Adams. Indeed his concern with appearances included a horror of appearing vain. He would not assist would-be biographers for fear, he confessed to a friend, of having "vanity or ostentation imputed to me."[18] He would not even allow Arthur Young, the great English agricultural reformer with whom he corresponded, to publish extracts from the letters, for fear of seeming ostentatious or of giving occasion for some "officious tongue to use my name with indelicacy."[19]

But if Washington was not vain, his very fear of appearing so argues that he did care deeply about what people thought of him. Although honor was in part a private matter, a matter of maintaining one's self-respect by doing right regardless of what the world demanded, it was also a matter of gaining the respect of others. Washington wanted respect, and he sought it first where men have often sought it, in arms.

The story of his youth is familiar, how his older brother Lawrence returned from the siege of Cartagena to fill young George with dreams of military glory. We see him at the age of twenty-one leading an expedition to the Ohio country and the next year another one, in which he fired the opening shots in the final struggle between France and Britain for the American continent. From the outset he made it plain that he was in search of honor. A letter penned at his camp in the Ohio country informed the governor of Virginia in words that Washington would later have eschewed as ostentatious, "the motives that lead me here were pure and noble. I had no view of acquisition, but that of Honour, by serving faithfully my King and Country."[20] Military honor seemed to Washington to be worth any sacrifice. "Who is there," he asked, "that does not rather Envy, than regret a Death that gives birth to Honour and Glorious memory?"[21]

But it was not necessary to die in order to win military honor. Armies were organized to express honor and respect every hour of the day, through the ascending scale of rank, from the lowliest private soldier up to the commander in chief. Officers often worried more about their rank than they did about the enemy. On his expedition against the French in 1754, Washington, along with other officers of the Virginia militia, was mortally offended by a captain in the British army who appeared on the scene and claimed to outrank all provincials, even those of a higher nominal grade. Washington later resigned his commission rather than submit to this kind of dishonor.[22] Thereafter he sought in vain for a royal commission in the regular British army in order to avoid such embarrassment. Failing to obtain one, he served again with the provincial troops when the Virginia frontier needed protection and provincial command was urged upon him, because he thought "it wou'd reflect eternal dishonour upon me to refuse it."[23]

Washington continued to regard rank as a matter of high importance. Throughout the Revolutionary War he had to press upon Congress the need for the utmost care and regularity in promotions in order to avoid offending officers who felt that they had not been given the grade they deserved. And the last years of his life were complicated by a dispute with John Adams over the order of rank in the general staff of the army that Congress created to prepare for war with France. But Washington recognized that an officer had to earn the respect that his rank entitled him to. And one of his ways of earning it was by cultivating the aloofness which became so marked a characteristic of his later years.

He may have begun with a large measure of native reserve, but he nourished it deliberately, for he recognized that reserve was an asset when you were in command of others. Mount Vernon, like other large plantations, was a school where the owner learned that giving orders and having them carried out were two different things. Slaves were in theory completely subject to the will of their master or overseer; but they were men, and like other men they gave obedience to those who could command their respect. And respect, in Washington's view, could not be won by familiarity. Familiarity bred contempt, whether in slaves or in soldiers.[24] Washington described the posture that he himself strove for in a letter of advice to a newly fledged colonel in the Continental Army. "Be easy and condescending in your deportment to your officers, but not too familiar, lest you subject yourself to a want of that respect, which is necessary to support a proper command."[25] With regard to enlisted men it was necessary to keep a still greater distance. Officers were supposed to be gentlemen, and they were expected to enhance the respect due them as officers by the respect due them as gentlemen. To make an officer of a man who was not a gentleman, a man who was not considered socially superior by his men, would mean, Washington said, that they would "regard him no more than a broomstick, being mixed together as one common herd."[26] Fraternizing with private soldiers was "unofficer and ungentlemanlike behaviour," cause for court-martial in Washington's army.[27] The commander in chief, then, must be all the more a figure apart, a figure to be respected rather than loved, a figure like the George Washington on whom so much honor was to be heaped and who, though without ostentation, dearly cherished the accolades.

Interest and honor, in Washington's view, were the springs that moved all men, including himself. And although the two might come in conflict and pull men in different directions, they need not do so. Often they were bound up together in curious ways. When Washington declared that he was seeking only honor in the Ohio country, he demonstrated that this was his motive by offering to serve without pay. But in making the offer he was trying to shame the Virginia assembly into giving provincial officers more pay. British officers got 22 shillings a day; Virginia was paying only 12 shillings 6 pence, and Virginia officers were accordingly resentful. But their resentment was not directed so much toward the pecuniary disadvantage as it was toward the implication that they were not as worthy as their British counterparts. It seemed so dishonorable not to be paid on the same scale that Washington would have preferred no pay at all. Interest and honor were intertwined.[28]

Interest and honor are likely to be linked in all public service. In seeking honor a man seeks the respect of others, of his family, of his social class, of his friends, his town, neighborhood, province, country. And people, however grouped, generally accord respect to someone who serves their interests. A man seldom looks for honor in promoting the interests of a group to which he does not belong. Consequently, in serving the interests of others he may well be serving his own, especially if he takes a large enough, long-range view.

How large a view Washington took before 1774 is not easy to assess. It certainly extended to the boundaries of Virginia, for he had served both in the colony's military and in the House of Burgesses. But his quest for a royal military commission looks like a yearning for rank, not for a larger sphere of action. It seems unlikely that Washington, any more than John Adams, would have expanded his horizons beyond his own province, had the colonies' quarrel with England not reached the boiling point. During the tumultuous decade before weapons replaced words, Washington imbibed the ideas of republican liberty that animated the spokesmen for American independence. He cannot properly be counted as one of those spokesmen. But he was convinced, long before the fighting began, that the English government was lost in corruption and was determined "by every piece of Art and despotism to fix the shackles of slavery upon us."[29] When Virginians sent him to the Continental Congress to join other Americans in resisting that threat, his horizons, like those of John Adams, expanded in the vision of a national republic. For the rest of his life, instead of serving only a county or province, he would serve a whole new nation. Honor and interest would remain the springs that moved him. But the honor and interest of George Washington somehow became the honor and interest of America.

To announce to the world the independence of Americans required daring, perhaps more so for Washington than for any of the other founding fathers, and perhaps more than he or they could have realized at the time. In accepting command of the as yet nonexistent Continental Army in June 1775, Washington staked his honor on defeating in battle the world's greatest military and naval power. And he staked it on behalf of a nation that was also as yet nonexistent. For a year he commanded a rebel army high in spirit and low on ammunition. By the time the great declaration turned the rebellion into a war for independence, the nation was materializing, and it would have been reasonable to expect that those who had embraced independence would rush to defend it with their lives and fortunes. But few Americans were yet as ready as Washington to face the meaning of independence. Washington found that he was in command of an army continually in the process of dissolution, and that he was under the direction of a Congress that grew increasingly shortsighted and timid, unwilling to take any steps that the fickle public might momentarily disapprove.

What was worse, the very cause in which he was embarked forbade him to take effective measures to remedy the situation. The republican liberty that Americans espoused required that the military be subject to the civil power, and Washington accepted the condition, even when the civil power became incompetent, irresponsible, and corrupt, even when he was obliged to share the blame for the errors of his congressional masters. He aimed at honor in the eyes of the people, but as a republican he could not attain his goal by appealing to the people over the heads of their elected representatives.[30]

The most he could do, while he tried to keep his army in being, was to point out to his masters with unwearying patience what experience had taught him but not them, namely that while men could be moved by honor, they could not be moved by it for long unless it marched hand in hand with interest. Washington had so fully identified his own interest and honor with the interest and honor of the new nation that he served without pay. But he knew that an entire army of men could not be sustained by honor alone. Enthusiasm for republican government would not alter human nature. Nor would it support a man's wife and children. If Congress could not make it in the interest of men to join the army and stay in the army, whether as enlisted men or as officers, the army could not last. Men had to be paid and paid enough to make it worth their while to face the hardships of military life while their neighbors stayed home. Washington acknowledged that men would fly readily to arms to protect their rights—for a short time, as they turned out to drive the British from Concord and Lexington. "But after the first emotions are over," Washington explained, "to expect, among such People, as compose the bulk of an Army, that they are influenced by any other principles than those of Interest, is to look for what never did, and I fear never will happen." And he went on to give the results of his own appeals to men to remain in the army for the honor of it. "A soldier reasoned with upon the goodness of the cause he is engaged in, and the inestimable rights he is contending for, hears you with patience, and acknowledges the truth of your observations, but adds that it is of no more Importance to him than others. The Officer makes you the same reply, with this further remark, that his pay will not support him, and he cannot ruin himself and Family to serve his Country, when every Member of the community is equally Interested and benefitted by his labours."[31]

Washington was never able to persuade Congress to pay his officers what he thought they should get, nor was he able to persuade them to enlist men for long enough terms to give him the disciplined striking force that he needed to meet the British on equal terms. The result, as he continually lamented, was "that we have protracted the War, expended Millions, and tens of Millions of pounds which might have been saved, and have a new Army to raise and discipline once or trice a year and with which we can undertake nothing because we have nothing to build upon, as the men are slipping from us every day by means of their expiring enlistments."[32] For a man in search of honor it was difficult to bear. The public blamed him for not taking action against the enemy, and he was unable even to explain to them why he did not. To have done so would have been to explain to the enemy how weak he was and thus invite an attack he was not equipped to repel.[33]

It hurt his sense of honor, too, to have to rely so heavily on the French. At the beginning of the war Washington had not expected much help from the French. He thought that they would supply him with arms and ammunition in return for the trade they would gain, and in order to annoy the British. But he had not counted on military assistance and would have been happier to win without it.[34] In the end French troops and the French navy were essential to his victory for the simple reason that the states would not field a large enough force themselves, even though he was persuaded that they could have done so.

The victory, nevertheless, was his. For eight years he presided over an army that would have dissolved without him. He put up with militia who came and went like the wind. He put up with officers, commissioned by Congress, who scarcely knew one end of a gun from the other. He put up with a horde of French volunteer geniuses who all expected to be generals. He led men who had no food, no shoes, no coats, and sometimes no weapons. He silenced one mutiny after another. He prevented his unpaid officers from seeking to overturn the delinquent government. And he did it all with that aloof dignity which earned the awesome respect of those he commanded and earned him in victory the honor of the nation that had come into existence almost in spite of itself.

Washington valued his laurels. When he retired to private life at Mount Vernon, it was with full consciousness that any further ventures in public life might only diminish the honor that was now his. Far better, after so many years' service, to keep out of the political hurly-burly, and this he longed to do. There remained, however, a threat that could not merely diminish but perhaps destroy both the honor he had won for himself and the independence he had won for Americans. That could be the consequence if the republic which he had fought to bring into being should itself dissolve.

The threat stemmed from the weakness of the central government. Washington had worried about it all through the war. By 1778 it had become evident to him that the states were sending lightweight men to Congress while the heavyweights stayed at home. The result was that "party disputes and personal quarrels are the great business of the day whilst the momentous concerns of an empire . . . are but secondary considerations," that "business of a trifling nature and personal concernment withdraws their attention from matters of great national moment." He could not complain to the public, but he could to his friends in Virginia. "Where are our Men of abilities?" he asked George Mason. "Why do they not come forth to save their Country? let this voice my dear Sir call upon you, Jefferson and others." "Where?" he demanded of Benjamin Harrison, "is Mason, Wythe, Jefferson, Nicholas, Pendleton, Nelson, and another I could name [meaning Harrison himself]?" They had all, it seemed, deserted Congress for Virginia.[35]

Nor did the situation improve as the war dragged to a close, supported by French arms and French credit. While the state governments grew stronger, Congress seemed to hobble on crutches. All business, so far as Washington could see, was merely "*attempted, for it is not done, by a timid kind of recommendation from Congress to the States.*"[36] By the time peace came, he was convinced that a new constitution creating a more effective national government was necessary to replace the Articles of Confederation. But he was still a republican and knew that this would not be possible until the people of the United States felt, as he did, "that the honor, power, and true Interest of this Country must be measured by a Continental scale; and that every departure therefrom weakens the Union, and may ultimately break the band, which holds us together." To work for a more effective national government was, he believed, the duty of "every Man who wishes well to his Country, and will meet with my aid as far as it can be rendered in the private walks of life."[37]

To go beyond the private walks of life was more than his intention, and even there he was wary of becoming associated with any enterprise that might endanger his standing in the public mind. He was uneasy about his connection with the Society of the Cincinnati, the organization formed by the retired officers of his army. To his surprise it had drawn heavy public criticism as the entering wedge of aristocracy. Washington was so baffled by the criticism that he asked his friend Jefferson to explain it to him, which Jefferson did with his usual grace and tact. The principal trouble was that membership was to be hereditary; Washington therefore insisted that this aspect of the society be abandoned. When some branches of the society declined to give it up, Washington determined not to serve as its president or attend its meetings, even though he thought the public jealousy wholly unwarranted.[38]

Washington believed that as a private citizen pursuing his own interests he could still be working for the good of the nation. He engaged without a qualm in a scheme that would benefit him financially, while it bolstered American independence in a way that he thought was crucial. Before the Revolution he had begun investing heavily in lands in the Ohio country, where as a young man he had made his military debut. While war lasted, the country lay empty of white inhabitants save for a few hardy souls who dared brave the Indian raids organized by the English. With the coming of peace began a great folk exodus from the established regions of the East (mainly from Virginia) over the mountains into the empty West. Washington expected the stream to swell steadily with immigrants, who would leave the monarchical tyrannies of the Old World for the republican freedom of the New. "The bosom of America is open," he declared, to "the oppressed and persecuted of all Nations and Religions." "Let the poor, the needy and oppressed of the Earth, and those who want Land, resort to the fertile plains of our western country."[39]

It was an axiom of the eighteenth century that the strength of a country lay in its people, and Washington like other Americans wanted the country to grow as rapidly as possible. His only reservation about immigrants from Europe was that they not settle in a group and thus "retain the Language, habits and principles (good or bad) which they bring with them."[40] It was important that they become Americans. It was even more important that all who trekked over the mountains, whether immigrant or native-born, remain Americans and not slip either by inclination or by force under the dominion of England or Spain. Both countries had retained footholds in the West, and the rivers flowed relentlessly into the Mississippi toward Spanish territory. The easiest, cheapest mode of exporting whatever the people of the West produced would thus be to ship it downriver to New Orleans. Fortunately, as Washington saw it, the Spanish forbade such shipments, and the Continental Congress was in no position to secure the privilege for Americans, though settlers had no sooner arrived in the western country than they began to demand it.[41]

Washington was persuaded that the West would gravitate to Spain and Britain unless the people there were bound to the East by the only ties that could bind men over the long run, ties of interest. The way to hold them in the nation was by building canals that would give settlers on the Ohio River a shorter water route to the East than the long float down the Mississippi. Washington accordingly devoted his energies to promoting two companies that would build canals from the Ohio and the Great Kanawha to the heads of navigation on the Potomac and the James. "The consequences to the Union," he wrote to his friend James Warren, "in my judgment are immense . . . for unless we can connect the new States which are rising to our view in those regions, with those on the Atlantic by *interest,* (the only binding cement, and no otherwise to be effected but by opening such communications as will make it easier and cheaper for them to bring the product of their labour to our markets, instead of going to the Spaniards southerly, or the British northerly), they will be quite a distinct people; and ultimately may be very troublesome neighbors to us."[42]

It did not bother Washington that in pressing for these canals he was furthering his own speculative interests as well as those of the nation. But he was embarrassed when the Virginia legislature, in chartering the companies to carry out his project, awarded him 150 shares in them. How would this be viewed by the world, he asked himself. Would it not "deprive me of the principal thing which is laudable in my conduct?" Honor and interest could apparently run together if the only benefit he received from the project was an increase in the value of his western lands, but honor would depart if he profited directly from the enterprise he had advocated. On the other hand, if he declined to accept the gift, would it not appear to be an act of ostentatious righteousness? He escaped the dilemma by accepting the shares but donating them to the support of a school in Virginia and to the foundation of a national university, another project designed to foster national feeling. The future leaders of the nation assembled there as students from all parts of the country would learn to shake off their local prejudices.[43]

The canals were not completed in Washington's lifetime and could not fulfill the political function he envisaged for them. Moreover, the union was threatened more by the impotence of Congress than by the disaffection of western settlers. By the terms of the peace treaty, the British outposts in the Northwest should have been given over to the United States, but the British continued to hold them. They were also doing their best to hasten the expected collapse of the republic by refusing to allow American ships in the ports they controlled in the West Indies and elsewhere in the world. Congress, with no authority to regulate American trade, was unable to retaliate.

The debility of Congress seems to have bothered Washington as much for its damage to the nation's reputation abroad as for its depressing effects at home. To be unable to retaliate against the economic warfare of the country he had defeated in battle must render the nation "contemptable in the eyes of Europe."[44] Because he had identified his own honor so completely with that of the nation, the contempt of Europe touched him personally and deeply; and he felt the shame redoubled when the people of western Massachusetts broke out in rebellion and neither the state government nor the national government seemed able to cope with them. "For

God's sake," he wrote to his Connecticut friend David Humphreys, "tell me what is the cause of all these commotions; do they proceed from licentiousness, British-influence disseminated by the tories, or real grievances which admit of redress? If the latter, why were they delayed till the public mind had become so much agitated? If the former why are not the powers of Government tried at once?" Europeans had said right along that a republican government was incapable of the energy needed to support itself in an area as large as the United States. Now the Americans seemed bent on exemplifying the criticism. "I am mortified beyond expression," said Washington, "that in the moment of our acknowledged independence we should by our conduct verify the predictions of our transatlantic foe, and render ourselves ridiculous and contemptible in the eyes of all Europe."[45]

As the situation worsened, Washington argued among his friends for an extension of congressional power, but at the same time he despaired of its doing much good, for "the members [of Congress] seem to be so much afraid of exerting those [powers] which they already have, that no opportunity is slipped of surrendering them, or referring the exercise of them, to the States individually."[46] By 1786 he was convinced, rightly or wrongly, that the country was fast verging toward anarchy and confusion, to a total dissolution of the union. He thought that the convention called to meet at Philadelphia to recommend changes in the national government offered the only hope of rescue, but it seemed so forlorn a hope that he was wary of attending it. When elected as a delegate, he delayed his acceptance to the last minute.[47]

Washington was ready to do everything possible, he said, "to avert the humiliating and contemptible figure we are about to make in the annals of mankind."[48] He was alarmed to hear that otherwise respectable people were talking of a need for monarchical government, and he feared that his refusal to attend the convention might be interpreted "as dereliction to republicanism."[49] But on the other hand, if the effort to save the republican union failed, the persons who made the effort "would return home chagrined at their ill success and disappointment." "This would be a disagreeable circumstance for any one of them to be in," he said, "but more particularly so for a person in my situation."[50] His situation was unique. It was he, after all, more than any other man, who had won independence for the nation. If the nation proved unworthy of it and incapable of sustaining it, the fault would not be his. He would still retain something of the honor he had gained in the struggle, even though it would be sadly diminished. But if he associated himself with a losing effort to save what he had won, he would reduce still further the significance of his achievement.

In the end, of course, he went to the convention and inevitably was elected to preside over it. The constitution it produced, whatever its defects, seemed to him the best that could be obtained and its acceptance the only alternative to anarchy. He would not plead in public for its adoption, but to his friends he made plain his total support of it and his opposition to proposals for amending it before it was put in operation.[51] His friends in turn made plain that if it were adopted he would be called upon to serve as the first president.[52]

Again in terms of honor and interest Washington weighed the risks of accepting office. His inclination was to stay at Mount Vernon, to make the place more profitable and keep it looking the way he wanted it to. To preside over the new government "would be to forego repose and domestic enjoyment, for trouble, perhaps for public obloquy."[53] There would be no honor in presiding over a fiasco, and he suspected that there was a sinister combination afoot among the Antifederalists to defeat the effective operation of the new government if they should be unsuccessful in preventing its adoption. But if he should be convinced, he told his friend Henry Lee, that "the good of my Country requires my reputation to be put in risque, regard for my own fame will not come in competition with an object of so much magnitude."[54] The good of the country did require Washington to take the risk.

The good of the country, perhaps its very survival, required above all that its citizens should respect its government, that they should not regard it with the contempt that the state legislatures had shown for the Continental Congress. And no one else but Washington could have given the presidency and the new government the stature they attained by his mere presence. His own honor was already so great that some of it could flow from him to the office he occupied.

Not least of the assets he brought to the task was the commanding dignity that he had won by his deliberately cultivated aloofness, the posture that demanded respect and honor from those below him, magnified now by men's memories of his previous triumphs. There was no need for fancy titles. John Adams and the new Senate worried about how to address him, and to Washington's annoyance Adams made himself ridiculous by arguing for the exalted forms of address employed for the kings of European countries. Washington carried so much dignity in his manner that he required no title to convey it. Though he would not have consented to "Farmer George," he did not need "Your Highness." He nevertheless took his usual pains to avoid familiarity. In Washington's view, the president of the Continental Congress during the 1780s, by opening his doors to all comers, had diminished what little authority the Articles of Confederation allowed him and thus brought the office into contempt. Washington would be less available to every Tom, Dick, and Harry who wished to gawk at him.[55]

He would also keep his distance from the other branches of government. The absence of a strong executive branch had been one of the great weaknesses of the old government that the Constitution tried to remedy. But it was up to the new president to strengthen the new government by maintaining in full vigor all the powers that the Constitution assigned to his office. It was up to him to establish the separation of executive and legislative branches that the Constitution stipulated. That Washington succeeded is a matter of record.

While magnifying the role of the president in government was important to Washington, it seems to have come easily, one might say naturally, to him; and he actually concerned himself more with the international standing of the nation. Improving the strength and reputation of the United States in relation to other nations became his main focus. In this area his special view of human motives proved to be a special asset. His own concern with private interest and his conviction that this was the principal spring of human action had grown with time. And he saw, in the nations of the world, collections of men who had combined in their own interests and pledged their honor, as he had pledged his, to serve those interests. It was in vain, then, to appeal to the honor of any country against the interests of that country and of its people. Honor for a Frenchman lay in serving the interests of the French, as for an American it lay in serving the interests of Americans. Although Washington was convinced, like many men of his time, that the interests of different countries need not conflict, he was certain that no country would or ought to act against its own perceived interests. To expect any country to do so was folly, and it was criminal folly for any man charged with his country's interests to trust another country with them, as for example Congress had done in instructing its envoys to be directed by the French court in the peace negotiations with England.

Washington had first demonstrated the acuity of his understanding of the role of national interest in foreign relations during the war, when Congress developed an enthusiasm for an expedition against Canada to be conducted by French troops. Since Canada was populated mainly by Frenchmen, it was thought that a French invasion would have a much better chance of success than the disastrous expedition that the colonists themselves had mounted in the early months of the war. In the treaty of alliance with the United States, France had formally renounced any claim of its own on Canadian territory. If conquered, the area would belong to the United States. The prospect of French troops in Canada had nevertheless alarmed Washington. If the French wished to undertake the move, he was in no position to prevent them. Beggars could not be choosers. But he could plead.

He officially presented to Congress and to the French all the plausible tactical disadvantages he could think of against a Canadian expedition.[56] Then, in a confidential private letter to Henry Laurens, the president of the Continental Congress, he explained why the proposal disturbed him. It would mean, he said, "the introduction of a large body of French troops into Canada, and putting them in possession of the capital of that Province, attached to them by all the ties of blood, habits, manners, religion and former connexions of government. I fear this would be too great a temptation to be resisted by any power actuated by the common maxims of national policy." He went on to list the economic and political benefits that France would gain by holding the province in violation of the treaty. It would not be difficult to find a plausible pretext; Canada need only be claimed as a security for American payment of the large debt owed to France. "Resentment, reproaches, and submission" would be the only recourse for the United States. And Washington went on to read a gentle lecture to the gullible members of Congress: "Men are very apt to run into extremes," he said, "hatred to England may carry some into an excess of Confidence in France; especially when motives of gratitude are thrown into the scale. Men of this description would be unwilling to suppose France capable of acting so ungenerous a part. I am heartily disposed to entertain the most favourable sentiments of our new ally and to cherish them in others to a reasonable degree; but it is a maxim founded on the universal experience of mankind, that no nation is to be trusted farther than it is bound by its interest; and no prudent statesman or politician will venture to depart from it."[57]

Whether or not the French merited Washington's wariness had not been put to the test in 1779, for they had not seen fit to undertake the expedition to Canada, though they toyed with the idea. Distrust of foreign attachments nevertheless took firm root beside Washington's other political instincts, and during his years in command of the army and in retirement at Mount Vernon he had advocated a stronger national government, not merely to prevent internal dissolution but to keep the country from falling under the influence of one of the more energetic monarchies of the Old World. Early in 1788, when war clouds were gathering over Europe and the Constitution had not yet been ratified, he had written to Jefferson of his fear that the several states, uninhibited by any effective central direction, might be drawn into the European quarrels.[58]

As president, Washington was at last able to exercise control over foreign relations, and in doing so he never swerved from the maxim of national interest that he had sought to impress upon Henry Laurens. That maxim, as he interpreted it, dictated that apart from commercial transactions, the United States should have as little to do as possible with any other nation. The true interest of the United States consisted in staying clear of foreign alignments and supplying all sides with the products which its fertile lands could produce in abundance. If the United States could maintain a policy of strict neutrality, the endless wars of the European monarchs would serve both to advance the price of American products and to swell the stream of immigrants needed to fill the empty American West.[59] Accordingly, as the threatened European war became reality, it was Washington's consistent policy to build the power of the United States by asking no favors of foreign countries and giving none. The aloofness which he associated with command was the proper posture to give power and respectability to a nation as well as an individual.

Although Washington anticipated commercial benefits from this policy of neutrality, he did not think it wise in negotiating treaties to take undue advantage of the bargaining position offered to the United States by the distresses of other countries. In his view, since he believed nations acted always according to their interest, a treaty was useful only so long as its provisions coincided with the interests of both countries. In 1791 he warned Gouverneur Morris, before he appointed him United States minister to France, that it would be useless to obtain favorable treaties from countries in distress, "For unless treaties are mutually beneficial to the Parties, it is in vain to hope for a continuance of them beyond the moment when the one which conceives itself to be over-reached is in a situation to break off the connexion."[60] The treaty with England that ended the Revolutionary War was a case in point. Although Washington complained when the British broke it by carrying off slaves and by refusing to turn over the Northwest posts, he had not really expected them to act differently.[61] The Americans had obtained on paper an agreement that went beyond what their military power entitled them to. It was therefore to be expected that the agreement would be broken.

Washington's foreign policy has sometimes been judged by the two treaties he signed, one regarded as a diplomatic triumph, the other as a defeat. But Washington himself did not set much store by either of them. In Jay's Treaty with England the United States seemed to get much less than it might have, and Washington did not think the treaty a good one. But he thought it better than the uncertain conditions of trade that would have resulted from a refusal to ratify it.[62] If it gave Americans less than they wanted, that was because they did not yet have the bargaining power to demand more—or so at least it seemed to Washington. In Pinckney's Treaty with Spain, the United States got permission for settlers in the West to ship their goods through Spanish territory via the Mississippi. Although Washington in the 1780s had thought contact between the westerners and the Spanish undesirable, by the 1790s he was ready to insist on the American right to navigate the Mississippi. But he did so only because it had become apparent that a failure to demand the right would alienate the westerners from the national government more rapidly than the connection with Spanish New Orleans would. He had never doubted that the westerners would ultimately get the right, because they were growing in numbers so rapidly that it would not be within the power of the light Spanish forces at New Orleans to deny them for long. Pinckney's Treaty gave them only what they would have taken anyhow.[63]

Thus treaties in Washington's view were of little worth. If the interests of two nations happened to coincide, a treaty was scarcely necessary to bind them together. If their interests conflicted, no treaty would be sufficient to hold them. At best a treaty could only regularize and expedite friendly relations between two countries. At worst it might weaken a country by misleading unwary statesmen to act for the benefit of an ally without due regard to their own country's interest.[64]

The important thing, Washington believed, was for Americans to discern their own interest as a nation and to pursue it without trying to take advantage of other countries and without allowing other countries to take advantage of the United States. This was the message of his Farewell Address, both in the version drafted by James Madison in 1792 and in the much different final version drafted by Alexander Hamilton in 1796.[65] He put it more succinctly himself in a letter to William Heath in 1797: "No policy, in my opinion, can be more clearly demonstrated, than that we should do justice to *all* but have no political connexions with *any* of the European Powers, beyond those which result from and serve to regulate our Commerce with them. Our own experience (if it has not already had this effect) will soon convince us that *disinterested* favours, or friendship from any Nation whatever, is too novel to be calculated on; and there will always be found a wide difference between the words and actions of any of them."[66]

In staking his own honor on the pursuit of national interest, Washington did not come off unscathed. He had committed himself so closely to the nation and its government that every attack on government policies seemed to be an attack on him. And by the time he left office the attacks were coming thick and fast, including some that were openly directed at him, charging that he had deserted the republican faith and was squinting at monarchy. Although he professed to be unmoved by these diatribes, his friend Jefferson testified that "he feels these things more than any person I ever yet met with."[67] And because Jefferson himself was a critic of national policies, Washington could not dissociate Jefferson from the assaults.

Washington's last years were saddened by this seeming repudiation of him, but his republican trust in the ordinary man remained unshaken. Less than a year before his death in 1799 he was still affirming that "the great mass of our Citizens require only to understand matters rightly, to form right decisions."[68] And so far as his own honor was concerned, his faith was justified. The mass of citizens did not deny him in the end the full measure of honor that was due him. Nor did Jefferson, even though Jefferson thought it was the president rather than the people who needed to understand matters rightly. Fourteen years after Washington's death, Jefferson recalled how the president had often declared to him "that he considered our new Constitution as an experiment on the practicability of republican government, and with what dose of liberty man could be trusted for his own good; that he was determined the experiment should have a fair trial, and would lose the last drop of his blood in support of it."[69]

Although Jefferson feared that Washington's emphatic assertion may have hidden a waning confidence in the experiment, there is no evidence that this was the case. To the end Washington cherished his honor, and to the end his honor demanded the preservation of the American republic, free of every foreign connection. That was the meaning of independence for Washington. He was even ready, perhaps a little too ready, to don his old uniform and command a new army in the war with France that seemed so imminent in 1798. When he died the next year, he could not have been sure that his republic would in fact sustain its independence. And had he lived another year, he would have found little to cheer him in the election that elevated Jefferson to the presidency. But he need not have feared. The republic did survive and long preserved the aloofness from foreign quarrels that he had prescribed for it. His honor survived with it, and posterity has preserved his image in all the aloofness that he prescribed for himself. Although the mass of citizens have learned to look upon most of their other historical heroes with an affectionate familiarity, they have not presumed to do so with Washington. The good judgment that he was sure they possessed has prevented a posthumous repetition of the folly perpetrated by Gouverneur Morris. Americans honor the father of their country from a respectful distance. And that is surely the way Washington would have wanted it.

NOTES

1. Max Farrand, ed., *The Records of the Federal Convention of 1787* (New Haven, 1911), 3:85, 86n.

2. George Washington, *The Writings of George Washington from the Original Manuscript Sources, 1745–1799*, ed. John C. Fitzpatrick (Washington, D.C., 1931–44), 2:427–31, 442, 461–62, 490–91, 37:490–94. All pages and volume numbers in the notes to this chapter refer to this work, unless otherwise indicated.

3. See, for example, 27:2–3, 31:392. Washington followed the same policy in all his business dealings. As he put it to Richard Boulton, a carpenter hired to fix his roof: "I do not enter into agreements, but with an intention of fulfilling them; and I expect the same punctuality on the part of those with whom they are made: and you must therefore perform your's with me, or abide the consequences" (June 24, 1785, 28:175–76).

4. To George Muse, Jan. 29, 1774, 3:179–80. See also to John Price Posey, Aug. 7, 1782, 24:485–87; to Gilbert Simpson, Feb. 13, 1784, 27:329–30.

5. Vols. 32 and 33, passim.

6. To John Augustine Washington, Jan. 16, 1783, 26:43.

7. To Lund Washington, Dec. 10, 1776, 37:535.

8. To Anthony Whiting, Dec. 23, 1792, 32:276.

9. To Anthony Whiting, Feb. 17, 1793, 32:345–48.

10. To Anthony Whiting, April 21, 1793, 32:422–27.

11. To Anthony Whiting, Dec. 30, 1792, 32:279. See also 32:245–50, 257, 276, 282, 283, 293, 316–19, 330, 345–48, 356–59, 442–44, 33:395–96, 398–402, 34:135, 153–54.

12. 33:208–15 (quotations at pp. 210 and 213).

13. To James Anderson, May 22, 1798, 36:267–68.

14. 28:182–88, 394–95, 510–15, 29:296–300, 31:436–40, 32:196–97, 34:453ff., 35:500–501.

15. To William Woodford, Dec. 13, 1779, 17:254.

16. General Orders, Nov. 19, 1779, 17:137.

17. Letters to Tobias Lear, vol. 31, passim.

18. To Dr. James Craik, March 25, 1784, 27:371.

19. To Arthur Young, Dec. 4, 1788, 30:153. Cf. 28:35, 98–100.

20. To Robert Dinwiddie, May 29, 1754, 1:63.

21. To Mrs. George William Fairfax, Sept. 25, 1758, 2:293.

22. 1:74–84, 104–7.

23. To Mrs. Mary Washington, Aug. 14, 1755, 1:159; cf. 1:159–63.

24. To William Pearce, Dec. 18, 1793, Nov. 16, 1794, 33:194, 34:25.

25. To Colonel William Woodford, Nov. 10, 1775, 4:80–81. Cf. 3:508.

26. To President of Congress, Sept. 24, 1776, 6:106. See also to Patrick Henry, Oct. 5, 1776, 6:167.

27. 10:434, 473, 12:7, 22, 13:212.

28. 1:49, 59–67, 83.

29. To George William Fairfax, June 16, 1774, 3:221–26; to George Mason, April 5, 1769, 2:500–504; to Jonathan Boucher, July 3, 1770, 3:21; to Bryan Fairfax, July 4, 20, 1774, 3:227–29, 230–34; to John Augustine Washington, March 24, 1775, 3:277. See also to Bryan Fairfax, March 1, 1778, 11:2–5; to G. W. Fairfax, July 10, 1783, 27:57–60.

30. To President of Congress, Dec. 15, 1777, 10:159–60; to Lund Washington, Sept. 30, 1776, 6:136–38; to William Livingston, April 14, 1778, 11:256; to Virginia Board of War, Oct. 20, 1779, 16:495.

31. To President of Congress, Sept. 24, 1776, 6:107–8. See also to John Bannister, April 21, 1778, 11:286: "Men may speculate as they will; they may talk of patriotism; they may draw a few examples from ancient story, of great achievements performed by its influence; but whoever builds upon it, as a sufficient Basis for conducting a long and bloody War, will find themselves deceived in the end. We must take the passions of Men as Nature has given them, and those principles as a guide which are generally the rule of Action. I do not mean to exclude altogether the Idea of Patriotism. I know it exists, and I know it has done much in the present Contest. But I will venture to assert, that a great and lasting War can never be supported on this principle alone. It must be aided by a prospect of Interest or some reward. For a time, it may, of itself push Men to Action; to bear much, to encounter difficulties; but it will not endure unassisted by Interest."

32. To Fielding Lewis, July 6, 1780, 19:131.

33. To President of Congress, Feb. 18, 1776, 4:336: "to have the Eyes of the whole Continent fixed, with anxious expectation of hearing of some great event, and to be restrain'd in every Military Operation for want of the necessary means of carrying it on, is not very pleasing; especially, as the means used to conceal my weakness from the Enemy conceals it also from our friends and adds to their Wonder." See also to Patrick Henry, Nov. 13, 1777, 10:52.

34. To Richard Henry Lee, April 24, May 14, June 1, 1777, 7:463, 8:75,159; to John Augustine Washington, Aug. 5, 1777, 9:22; Circular to the States, Dec. 29, 1777, 10:222–23.

35. To Benjamin Harrison, Dec. 18, 1778, 13:467; to George Mason, March 27, 1779, 14:301.

36. To Fielding Lewis, July 6, 1780, 19:131.

37. To Lafayette, April 5, 1783, 26:298.

38. 27:388–89, 393–96, 28:350–52, 29:70–72, 113–16; Thomas Jefferson, *The Papers of Thomas Jefferson*, ed. Julian P. Boyd (Princeton, N.J., 1950–), 7:105–10.

39. To the members of the volunteer association and other inhabitants of the kingdom of Ireland who have lately arrived in the city of New York, Dec. 2, 1783, 27:254; to David Humphreys, July 25, 1785, 28:203. See also 28:206, 29:348–51, 356, 365, 504–5, 519–22. On Washington's awareness of the effect of the canals on the value of his lands, see his letter to the Countess of Huntington, Feb. 27, 1785, 28:86–89.

40. To John Adams, Nov. 15, 1794, 34:22–23. See also 28:69.

41. To President of Congress, Aug. 22, 1785, 28:230–31; to Secretary for Foreign Affairs, May 18, 1786, 28:460–61.

42. To James Warren, Oct. 7, 1785, 28:291. See also 27:471–80, 482–90, 28:3–5, 23–26, 48–55, 202–10, 230–33, 289–92, 29:35, 249–50.

43. 28:34–37, 77–81, 214–16, 303–4, 24:106–7, 146–51, 35:199.

44. To James Duane, April 10, 1785, 28:124; to William Grayson, Aug. 22, 1785, July 26, 1786, 28:233, 485–87; to David Humphreys, Oct. 22, 1786, 29:27.

45. To David Humphreys, Oct. 22, 1786, 29:27. See also 29:34, 51–52.

46. To William Grayson, Aug. 22, 1785, 28:234.

47. His hesitation was compounded by the fact that the Society of the Cincinnati was scheduled to meet in Philadelphia at the same time, and he had already declined to attend (29:70–72, 113–16, 119–20, 127, 151–53, 170–73, 177, 186–88).

48. To David Humphreys, Dec. 26, 1786, 29:128.

49. To the Secretary for Foreign Affairs, Aug. 1, 1786, 28:503; to Henry Knox, March 8, 1787, 29:170–71.

50. To David Humphreys, Dec. 26, 1786, 29:128.

51. To Lafayette he wrote, Sept. 18, 1787, "What will be the General opinion on, or the reception of it, is not for me to decide, nor shall I say anything for or against it: if it be good I suppose it will work its way good; if bad it will recoil on the Framers." But on Oct. 15 he wrote to Henry Knox that he thought the opponents of it were "governed by sinister and self important motives" (29:277, 289; see also 29:278, 309–13, 323, 340, 357–58, 372–73, 399, 409–12, 464–67).

52. 29:464–67, 479, 30:98, 110–12.

53. To Benjamin Lincoln, Oct. 26, 1788, 30:119.

54. To Henry Lee, Sept. 22, 1788, 30:98.

55. Queries, May 10, 1789, 30:319–21; to David Stuart, July 26, 1789, 30:359–66.

56. To President of Congress, Nov. 11, 1778, 13:223–44.

57. To Henry Laurens, Nov. 14, 1778, 13:254–57.

58. Jan. 1, 1788, 29:350–51. See also Circular to the States, June 8, 1783, 26:486; to John Augustine Washington, June 15, 1783, 27:12–13.

59. To Jefferson, Jan. 1, 1788, 29:350–51; to Lafayette, Aug. 11, 1790, 31:87.

60. July 28, 1791, 31:328. See also to same, March 25, 1793, 32:402–3: "this Country is not guided by such narrow and mistaken policy as will lead it to wish the destruction of any nation, under an idea that our importance will be increased in proportion as that of others is decreased. We should rejoice to see every nation enjoying all the advantages that nature and it's circumstances would admit, consistent with civil liberty, and the rights of other nations. Upon this ground the prosperity of this country would unfold itself every day, and every day would it be growing in political importance."

61. To President of Congress, Aug. 22, 1785, 28:231. See also 28:9–12.

62. 34:244, 237–40, 254–57, 262–64, 310–11.

63. See references in notes 41 and 42 and 30:486–87, 31:87.

64. 35:56–57.

65. Ibid. and 35:214–38.

66. May 20, 1797, 35:449.

67. To James Madison, June 9, 1793, Thomas Jefferson, *The Writings of Thomas Jefferson*, ed. Andrew A. Lipscomb and Albert E. Bergh (Washington, D.C., 1903–4), 9:120.

68. To James Lloyd, Feb. 11, 1799, 37:129.

69. To Walter Jones, Jan. 2, 1814, Jefferson, *Writings*, ed. Lipscomb and Bergh, 14:51.

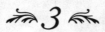

THOMAS JEFFERSON

THOMAS JEFFERSON HAS ALWAYS INVITED CONTROVERSY. Although he was a man of extraordinarily mild temper, much more so than either of our two previous subjects, although he himself abhorred controversy and refrained from answering most of the public attacks made on him during his lifetime, opponents sprang up wherever he went: a Patrick Henry in Virginia, an Alexander Hamilton in New York and Philadelphia, a John Marshall in Washington, and hired political hacks and newspaper scribblers everywhere.

He still has his opponents, and though I am not one of them, it is only fair to admit at the outset that some of them, in his own time and in ours, have had valid grounds for criticism. While he avoided open controversy, he did have a tendency, not unlike that of John Adams, to believe worse of his enemies than they deserved. Although it has been demonstrated that Jefferson's suspicions of Hamilton's connivance with the British were only too well founded,[1] Jefferson's views of both Hamilton and the British did sometimes verge on the paranoid. He filled his notebooks and autobiography with every rumor peddled to him about Hamilton as a king lover, a monarchist, a Tory. So convinced was he of Hamilton's hostility to the principles of the Revolution that he ascribed to him a cryptoloyalism during the Revolution itself, assigning him the authorship of the pamphlet *Plain Truth*, which was written in answer to Thomas Paine's *Common Sense* by a genuine loyalist, James Chalmers.[2] Jefferson was convinced that Hamilton and the Federalists planted attacks on George Washington in the newspapers, so phrased as to make them appear to come from the Republicans.[3] As for the British, not only did he credit them with controlling the Federalists and everything the Federalists did, but he also held them responsible for all the excesses of the French Revolution. After that Revolution had gone sour and drenched Europe with blood, Jefferson persuaded himself that the reign of terror and all the outrages committed by Danton, Marat, and Robespierre were instigated by British emissaries who had infiltrated the Jacobin societies as agents provocateurs.[4]

Given the extent of international intrigue that has now been authenticated for the late eighteenth century, it is perhaps uncharitable to dismiss such charges as the work of an overheated imagination. But Jefferson had other demerits not easy to overlook, especially at the present time. If his attitude toward the British verged on the paranoid, his attitude toward black slavery verged on hypocrisy. He repeatedly expressed his detestation of slavery and his willingness to support any feasible plan to eradicate the institution in Virginia and the United States. But he did not direct his considerable energies toward that end, nor did he get beyond wishful thinking in any of his plans to eliminate his dependence on a way of living that, by his own statement, deserved the wrath of God. He lived from the labor of slaves, and he lived well. He insisted that he was in agony until he could get out of debt and thus, having paid off his creditors, be able to pay his debts of freedom to the men and women who worked for him. But he never got out of debt and never tried very hard to do so. If his actions are any evidence, he placed a higher value on collecting books and drinking good wine than he did on freeing his slaves. The fact that he also believed in the racial inferiority of blacks and the impossibility of black and white living side by side in freedom does not make his acquiescence in slavery more palatable. And his view that extending slavery across the continent would somehow dilute the evil of it strikes one as the shallowest kind of sophistry.[5] Thomas Jefferson is not likely to win many friends today among blacks.

Nor is he likely to look very attractive to any modern feminists who read his writings. Though I do not recall having seen any attacks on him from this quarter as yet, they are sure to come. For Jefferson had the patronizing attitude of the eighteenth-century southern gentleman toward women. They were lovely companions, deserving all the tenderness that one could give them. But their place was in the home, looking after the household. In France, like Franklin, he made friends with several charming French ladies who ventured often outside the household, not to mention the bewitching Maria Cosway, with whom, forgiving her English birth, he seems to have fallen in love. But he no more approved of the delightful women of Europe than did John Adams. He revealed his attitude in the lecture he read Anne Willing Bingham, the beautiful wife of an ambitious Philadelphia merchant, about the dangerous proclivity of French women to delve into politics. Jefferson was sure, he said, that America's good ladies "have been too wise to wrinkle their foreheads with politics. They are contented to soothe and calm the minds of their husbands returning ruffled from political debate."[6] He also assured Angelica Schuyler Church that she need not be agitated by the controversy over ratification of the Constitution in New York, because "the tender breasts of ladies were not formed for political convulsion; and the French ladies miscalculate much their own happiness when they wander from the true field of their influence into that of politicks."[7] Twenty years later his views had not changed. When it was suggested to President Jefferson that women might be capable of holding public office, he branded the idea as an "innovation for which the public is not prepared," and added, "nor am I."[8]

Jefferson's well-known prejudice against cities and city people extended to women who were brought up in them. Giving his sister-in-law advice about her son, he urged her not to let him fall in love in Philadelphia, because, he said, "I know no such useless bauble in a house as a girl of mere city education."[9] Presumably part of the trouble was that in Philadelphia and other cities of the North well-bred young girls got more schooling than was common in rural Virginia, and thereby acquired too great a penchant for reading. Jefferson, who could not live without books himself, had a low opinion of their value for women. When his daughter Martha was about to present him with his first grandchild, he congratulated her on the new domestic chores she would be gaining and added, perhaps as an admonition, "as to reading it is useful for only filling up the chinks of more useful and healthy occupations."[10]

One could doubtless find other shortcomings in Jefferson, as many of his critics have, but in trying to assess the meaning of American independence for the man who wrote the declaration proclaiming it, I find his attitudes toward blacks and toward women the most disturbing. Not that he differed markedly in these attitudes from other people of his time and place, though even then his friend Abigail Adams would have been able to straighten him out about a few things. What is disturbing is that Jefferson was not ahead of his time in these areas, because in most questions relating to human dignity, and especially in the devising of ways to protect and nourish human dignity, Jefferson *was* ahead of his time and ahead of ours. He was *not* ahead in thinking about black slavery or in thinking about women, and we shall simply have to admit that and get on with learning what he still has to teach. My way of trying to do that is to examine the meaning of independence for him as I have examined it for John Adams and George Washington.

With Jefferson it is difficult to discover personal qualities transformed by the Revolution into something larger. Jefferson had none of the vanity of a John Adams to be transformed into national ambition. Nor did he have Washington's strong attachment to private interest or any apparent yearning for public honor. Jefferson's personal qualities are, in fact, not easy to uncover. Those who have studied him have often observed the elusiveness of his personality. Although he was continually in company and could talk brilliantly with visitors about virtually any topic they brought up, he did not talk much about himself. His private life was so private that those who have tried to penetrate it have had to rely on tenuous connections and conjectures. This very reserve, this privacy may perhaps be a clue to the meaning of independence for Jefferson. But there are others, more obvious, to be examined first.

To begin with, it will be worth reminding ourselves that Jefferson, like Washington and Adams, was devoted to the nation and the national government that he and they did so much to create. Like Washington, he was eager to teach his fellow Virginians to be less provincial, to see things from a national perspective.[11] Although he is regularly hailed as a champion of states' rights against the national government (which he was), he was also an ardent advocate of strengthening the national government at the time when it needed strengthening. When the Continental Congress sent him to Europe in 1784 to negotiate commercial treaties, he went prepared to use treaty making as a means of extending the power of the feeble Congress. The Articles of Confederation gave Congress no authority to regulate trade but did confer the power to make treaties. Commercial treaties could thus be the instrument of trade regulation. The scheme proved unworkable for the very reason that prompted it: European countries would not risk a commercial treaty with a government that had no authority to regulate the trade of its own citizens.[12] The states of Europe were in fact reluctant to cooperate with the new American republic about anything, even when it seemed to Jefferson clearly in their interest to do so. They turned a cold shoulder, for example, to an obviously sensible scheme he concocted to protect shipping in the Mediterranean by means of a multinational patrol against the Barbary pirates. When the European states refused the joint operation, Jefferson was eager for the United States to build a fleet and do the job alone.[13]

Jefferson urged the creation of a navy at this time not simply because he thought it was shameful for American ships and American citizens to be at the mercy of a handful of seagoing bandits. He believed also that a navy would help to strengthen the hand of Congress. "It will be said," he admitted, "there is no money in the treasury. There never will be money in the treasury till the confederacy shews it's teeth. The states must see the rod; perhaps it must be felt by some one of them."[14] A navy would be a smart rod, for, as James Madison had earlier suggested to him, "A single frigate under the orders of Congress could make it the interest of any one of the Atlantic States to pay its quota."[15] Jefferson pressed the idea on John Adams, but even Adams, the champion of naval power, thought the expense of a navy would be at this point too great for the Congress to bear.[16] After the Constitution conferred the power to tax on the national government, Jefferson tried again, as secretary of state, to commit the United States to a naval war against the Barbary States that sponsored piracy in the Mediterranean;[17] but it was not until he became president himself that he could move the country toward substituting bombardment and broadsides for the tribute that other nations paid for safe passage of their ships.

Jefferson's aggressive concern for the nation also found early expression in his attitude toward the European powers that held land adjacent to the United States. He tended to think of North America, if not the whole New World, as belonging of right to the United States. And he was confident that the United States must be "the nest from which all America, North and South is to be peopled."[18] In 1788 he assured William Carmichael, the United States envoy to Spain, that America would not support any efforts by other countries to subvert Spanish possessions in the New World. Spain ought to see, he said, that "her views and ours must, in a good degree, and for a long time, concur." But poor Carmichael must have felt some embarrassment if he tried to explain Jefferson's reasoning to the Spanish. For Jefferson wanted Spain to keep its possessions only because Spain was weak, and when the United States was ready to expand, it would be easier to wrest territory from a weak country than from a strong one.[19] In his plans for westward expansion he was prepared, at one time, to claim the right to navigate the Mississippi to its mouth because Americans held its upper reaches, and he was prepared at another time to claim dominion over the upper reaches of the Columbia River (and perhaps a good deal more) because Americans occupied its mouth.[20]

Jefferson was even more of an isolationist than Washington was, and he held an even lower opinion of treaties. Although most Americans associate with Washington's farewell address the phrase "entangling alliance," the words actually come from Jefferson's first inaugural address. Not only did Jefferson want no alliances, he probably would have taken any opportunity of excluding European countries from the whole Western hemisphere. Failing that, he developed the principle of "no transfer," which ultimately became known as the Monroe Doctrine, interdicting European exchanges of New World territory.[21] In a word, Jefferson was devoted to the American nation, devoted to its growth, ever eager to strengthen it, and jealous of any European country that came near it. By no accident his presidency saw the territory under American control double in size.

To argue that such a man lacked an understanding of political power would be foolish. People who lack such an understanding are not likely to reach the presidency of the United States. Jefferson became president because in some ways he understood power and the popular roots of power better than John Adams or Alexander Hamilton. In the course of his career he also demonstrated again and again a keen perception of the way power politics operated internationally. And yet, despite the conscientiousness with which he carried out every office in which power was conferred on him, Jefferson was not at his best in exercising power. His record as governor of Virginia was no more than defensible and required defending. As secretary of state, he was regularly outmaneuvered by Hamilton, and he resigned the office at a time when it might still have furnished a potent means to deflect policies of which he disapproved. As president he made in the embargo his boldest bid to coerce England and France into recognizing American rights. But he was obliged to give it up when a handful of Federalists overturned a Republican Congress that Jefferson would probably have been able to control if he had tried hard enough. The fact is that Jefferson, for all his understanding of power and for all the time he spent in the seats of power, was not good at using it and did not enjoy using it. "I have never been so well pleased," he confessed in 1811, "as when I could shift power from my own, on the shoulders of others."[22]

A wish to shift power to others was a matter of personal inclination, but Jefferson was reluctant not only to use power but to have it used. He distrusted power, and we shall miss the meaning of independence for him if we see his devotion to the American nation as simply a devotion to the power and spread of its government. Governments by definition were in the business of exercising power, and Jefferson's distrust of power extended to government. He made a point of distinguishing the nation from its government, a distinction that is implicit in the Declaration of Independence and that Jefferson stated explicitly at least as early as 1787.[23] He developed it more fully when called upon to decide whether the United States treaty with France was rendered void by the change in the French government with the end of the monarchy. The United States government changed in 1789, but the nation remained. The French government changed in 1792, but the nation remained. The nation was the source of authority and might employ any government it chose.[24] Jefferson's national loyalty lay in a devotion to the American nation, not to the national government it employed.

Jefferson had reasons, beyond the accident of being born in America, for his attachment to the nation and his eagerness to see it grow. His stay in France enabled him to compare his own nation with another. He found in France much to admire that was missing in America: the food, the wine, the architecture, the painting, the music, and the polite manners of the people, whose "little sacrifices of self . . . really render European manners amiable, and relieve society from the disagreeable scenes to which rudeness often exposes it."[25] But between his uncouth countrymen and the amiable French there remained another difference that outweighed all the advantages that the French could claim. Americans, in the course of a century and a half of isolation from the Old World, had learned to govern themselves. In the absence of kings and aristocrats they had learned that men can live safely without them. And the kind of life they were thereby able to live was filled with greater happiness than could be found anywhere else on the face of the earth.

The governments that most European nations employed were, in Jefferson's view, governments of hawks over pigeons, of wolves over sheep.[26] And Jefferson was persuaded that their improvement could be brought about only gradually. A nation, it seemed, required time, more than a generation, to learn to live without wolves or hawks. During his lifetime he saw many attempts, all of which he welcomed and encouraged, but without great expectations of the outcome over the short run. In 1786, well before the French Revolution began, he wrote George Wythe of the "ignorance, superstition, poverty and oppression of body and mind" that prevailed among the mass of the people in Europe. "If all the sovereigns of Europe," he wrote, "were to set themselves to work to emancipate the minds of their subjects from their present ignorance and prejudices, and that as zealously as they now endeavor the contrary, a thousand years would not place them on that high ground on which our common people are now setting out."[27]

When the first stirrings of the French Revolution began in 1787 with the Assembly of Notables, Jefferson urged Lafayette and his friends to attempt no more than a constitutional monarchy on the English model, because that was the most that the French people were capable of until they gained more political experience. As the movement developed, he repeated the advice but expressed his own fear that "an impatience to rectify everything there at once" would lead to disaster.[28] A quarter century later, after a whole succession of disasters, he recalled his earlier warnings and concluded that the constitution established in 1818 offered France "as much self-government as perhaps she can bear."[29] Liberty, he felt, if obtained through force or accident by an "unprepared people" would quickly become "a tyranny still, of the many, the few, or the one."[30] He saw no brighter hopes for the Latin American colonies of Spain than for France. The people of Latin America were so oppressed and priest-ridden, so inexperienced in governing themselves, that as they revolted they would all fall prey to their "respective Bonapartes."[31] When Alexander of Russia showed signs of wishing to bring liberty there, Jefferson was equally pessimistic about the possibility of "securing freedom and happiness to those who are not capable of taking care of themselves."[32]

Americans, then, were a rather special people, almost the only people in the world, it would seem, who could take care of themselves, the only people ready for full self-government and for freedom from "this class of human lions, tygers and mammouts [mammoths] called kings."[33] No wonder that Jefferson should be attached to such a nation. No wonder he should be eager to see it extended. No wonder he should be proud to have written the document by which it affirmed its independence.

But to say this much and no more would be still to offer a travesty of what independence meant to Jefferson. I have said that he revered the nation, not the nation's government or governments. But the nation, even the American nation, did not hold for him the mystic aura that enters into what we usually call nationalism. He reserved his highest reverence not for the nation but for the individuals who comprised it. In a sense, he was as eager to free individuals from the pressures of the nation as he was to free the nation from the trammels of excess government; for the sake of the nation he was willing to play the state governments against the national government in order to hold both within their proper limits; and he was unperturbed by the thought of fracturing the nation itself for the benefit of the individuals in it.

We may get a hint of his attitude in his consistent support of those Americans who left the East Coast to search for a better life in the West. As a Virginian, Jefferson was ready to give up Virginia's enormous western territory rather than have the people in such a huge area be subject to a state government dominated by easterners, and he took the same position in relation to the control of westerners by a national government in which they would be no more adequately represented. The question to be answered in breaking up the West into new states, he argued, was not how to derive the maximum benefit either to the existing states or to the nation as a whole. The question was: "How may the territories of the Union be disposed of so as to produce the greatest degree of happiness to their inhabitants?"[34] Westerners were Americans, capable of self-government, and Jefferson thought they deserved the same freedom of political choice as other Americans, including the freedom to go their own way out of the union if they elected to do so. When he arranged for the purchase of Louisiana and New Englanders in Congress objected that settlers there would be so remote that they might eventually secede from the nation, Jefferson was unmoved. The settlers, he pointed out, would be the children and grandchildren of people in the East. "And if," he asked, "they see their interest in separation, why should we take side with our Atlantic rather than our Missipi [*sic*] descendants? . . . God bless them both, and keep them in union, if it be for their good, but separate them if it be better."[35] These are scarcely the words of an ardent nationalist in the usual sense. They are the words of a man who cared more about his fellow man than he did about the nation or national interest or national honor.

Jefferson's affirmation of a freedom of political choice for westerners was no more than what he affirmed for other men. In 1774, in the *Summary View of the Rights of British America* he reminded George III that the first English settlers of the New World had "possessed a right, which nature has given to all men, of departing from the country in which chance, not choice has placed them." In 1776 he wrote into the revised Virginia code of laws an expression of the right to emigrate, and he recurred to it often, as in negotiating the consular convention with France in 1784 and in agreements in the 1790s for extradition of criminals.[36] Jefferson thought it only proper that persons convicted of murder should be subject to extradition, but that was the only crime for which he would allow it, and he specifically denied it for treason, because "the unsuccessful strugglers against tyranny have been the chief martyrs of treason laws in all countries." A man had a right to escape from a country whose government he had tried in vain to improve.[37]

As well as offering asylum to such men, Jefferson thought that the governments of the United States, whether state or national, should look indulgently upon challenges to their own authority. Washington and Adams had both been upset by Shays's Rebellion. Not Jefferson. Since he valued the individual above government, he thought it should be a matter of pride for a government to have citizens willing to rebel. A rebellion constituted "proof that the people have liberty enough." The true strength of a government might thus be demonstrated by its weakness. Occasional rebellions might even be "a medicine necessary for the sound health of government," necessary in order to remind a government that it was not sacred.[38]

The individual came first, governments and nations a poor second. And yet not all individuals came first in Jefferson's conception of political rights. Even while affirming the right of expatriation, Jefferson negotiated the return from Spanish Florida of runaway slaves, who had committed neither murder nor treason and who, of course, had no political rights.[39] And his solicitude for the individual did not extend to the mechanics in America's cities, whom he classed with slaves and Frenchmen and Latin Americans as incapable of or unprepared for self-government. Who, then, were the individuals whose happiness Jefferson placed above the nation and the national government, and how did he propose to advance their happiness? In the answer to these questions lies finally the meaning of independence for Jefferson.

The individuals whom Jefferson cherished were those who had made the independence of the nation possible, those who were themselves already independent and capable of self-government. They were the landholding, literate farmers who constituted the great majority of the adult male population of the United States. Men who owned land on which to support themselves could bid defiance to the efforts of would-be tyrants to manipulate them. Their land conferred on them an independence that made them capable of self-government. "Those who labour in the earth," he said in a famous passage, "are the chosen people of God," and they were certainly the chosen people of Thomas Jefferson. "Generally speaking," he declared, "the proportion which the aggregate of the other classes of citizens bears in any state to that of its husbandmen, is the proportion of its unsound to its healthy parts." The great thing about the United States was that its healthy proportion was so large.[40]

In fastening on farmers as the healthy part of a state, Jefferson touched an old but lively tradition of political thought. Aristotle had first associated democracy with farming, and in seventeenth-century England James Harrington had given new life to the view by making a population of independent, armed landowners the sine qua non of a republic and the principal bulwark against tyranny in any state.[41] Eighteenth-century political thinkers had carried on the tradition. The ideal of the independent man as the source of liberty in the state was, as a perceptive historian has noted, "one of the few subjects on which the age allowed itself to become fanatical."[42]

Jefferson was himself almost fanatical about it, but his fanaticism took a turn that marks him off from other political thinkers of the time. Political thinkers, perhaps by definition, give their attention to the state and its government. Eighteenth-century thinkers were deeply concerned with liberty and with the organization of society and government to ensure it. The independent individual was a principal means to that end as well as the beneficiary of it. But for most political thinkers liberty was the attribute of a proper state with a proper government. Liberty was embedded in institutions, in the separation of powers, in trial by jury, in the writ of habeas corpus; and a body of independent citizens was needed to see that these were not subverted by ambitious rulers. Jefferson, too, believed in the importance of institutions, but for Jefferson liberty was always an attribute of the individual, and the state at best a means of securing it. The independence of the individual was not for Jefferson a means to an end so much as the end itself, to be sought by every possible means.

The difference was one of emphasis, but as in theology so in political thought: differences of emphasis can become the source of radical heresies. And Jefferson became so much of a heretic in political thought that many of his favorite schemes for bolstering the independence of the individual have never been tried. The exciting thing about the independence of the United States for him was not the creation of a new nation but the opportunity it offered to carry the independence of the individual beyond what the world had hitherto known. Jefferson would have been happy to see the individuals of other nations move toward the degree of independence that the majority of American men already enjoyed. He hoped that the slaves of America would also move or be moved in that direction. But what excited him was the cutting edge of independence, the further emancipation of the already free, the progress in individual independence of that majority of Americans who were already ahead of the rest of the world.

So jealous was he of the position Americans had attained that he was fearful about admitting large numbers of immigrants, who might jeopardize American progress. His belief in the right of expatriation forbade him any effort to exclude immigrants, but where Washington was eager to encourage them, in order to add to the nation's strength, Jefferson worried that they would bring with them the monarchical and aristocratic prejudices of the Old World and thus weaken the capacity of Americans to sustain their freedom and advance in it.[43]

Implicit in Jefferson's view of progress in independence was the recognition, already noted, that progress in independence must be slow. Slaves and European peasants would have to move in stages toward freedom, for men could move forward only from the position to which the preceding generation had brought them. Nations, if unprepared, could not hope to imitate the success of the American Revolution. And even in America only adequate education could bring men to the starting point for progress and preserve them from retrogression. Men must learn everything that their fathers had to teach. And the farther the people of a nation progressed, the more there was to learn. Jefferson continually urged his countrymen to expand their schools. Americans, having come into full control of their lives, must not slip backward. The human condition was so beset with perils that real effort would be required simply to stand still, and even greater effort to move forward. For when men proposed to move forward, they often found themselves fettered to the past. The past could be tyrant as well as teacher, binding men in institutional chains of ancient origin. But Jefferson was optimistic that in a nation where education was widespread and men were free to exercise their reason, they would be able to make a discriminating evaluation of the good and the bad in their inheritance and would take measures to discard whatever hindered the progress of independence.[44]

In trying to advance independence, they would have to contend with men who were dead set against progress. The world was full of men Jefferson described as "anti-philosophers, who find an interest in keeping things in their present state, who dread reformation, and exert all their faculties to maintain the ascendancy of habit over the duty of improving our reason, and obeying its mandates."[45] These were the people who insisted that what was good enough for their fathers was good enough for them. They were the Tories, the Federalists, who "fear and distrust the people, and wish to draw all powers from them into the hands of the higher classes."[46] They could be found in any society at any time, and in most societies they had managed to gain the upper hand and to lock their countrymen into laws and institutions that bound them to a benighted past and made them easy to exploit. Jefferson set his course against them in the American Revolution and in ensuing years devised a succession of schemes and programs to advance the independence of Americans against them. He liked to think of generations as nations, and he sought the independence not merely of Americans from England but of every generation of Americans from the preceding one. At the risk of putting words in the mouth of a man who could speak quite well enough for himself, I would say that Jefferson's public career focused on securing for Americans a right of expatriation from the past.

The Revolution, in Jefferson's view, gave Americans a rare chance to eliminate every inherited institution by which the old colonial governments had inhibited the pursuit of happiness. Those governments had perhaps contained more good than bad. Under them Americans had learned to govern themselves and to nourish the very ideas of freedom that would now enable them to win still greater freedom. But pride in the good must not be allowed to blind them to the need to hold every institution up to the lamp of republican liberty and decide whether or not it was worth keeping. Jefferson responded to the challenge first with a revisal of Virginia's laws, examining every statute from the colonial period to see whether it could still serve independent Americans.[47] In the process he saw to the abolition of primogeniture and entail. He perhaps attached a greater importance to this reform than it deserved, but it had a symbolic value, denying to any man the power to determine in perpetuity how his property should descend among future generations. And it was designed to multiply in the future the proportion of independent landholders.[48] Jefferson insisted too that the English common law, which had formerly prevailed in American courts, should henceforth be valid only insofar as specific doctrines of it were adopted by American legislatures.[49] There was much that he would keep, but only after a deliberate positive decision by the representatives of the people who would be affected. There had not been and could not have been even a "virtual representation" of independent Americans in the courtrooms where their English ancestors developed the common law.

A measure in which Jefferson took sufficient pride to have it engraved on his tombstone was the Virginia Act for Religious Liberty. This too he conceived as a means of freeing men from the dead hand of the past. Jefferson, like many other eighteenth-century thinkers, regarded the church as one of the institutions by which aristocrats and kings used the past to dominate the present. When he visited Milan, the cathedral there seemed to him "a worthy object of philosophical contemplation" only as a prime example of the misuse of money; and his contemplation prompted him to the observation that the capital spent in building all the churches of Italy "would have sufficed to throw the Appennines into the Adriatic and thereby render it terra firma from Leghorn to Constantinople," an enterprise which he evidently would have considered more worthwhile than the building of churches.[50] Although he counted himself an admirer of Jesus Christ, he thought the church and its priests were a principal obstacle to progress everywhere outside the United States. Wherever the church was supported by the state, it had a vested interest in preventing men from using their reason and relied on compulsion rather than persuasion to perpetuate itself. In Virginia as in the rest of the United States, outside New England, the fangs of the clergy had been drawn by the cessation of state support after the Revolution. As a result, when considering further reforms for Virginia late in life, Jefferson favored removing the prohibition in the state constitution against clergymen holding political office. Clergymen were individuals too, and since they had come to rely on voluntary support, on persuasion rather than force, they should not be penalized for the misbehavior of their predecessors. They too should be freed from the past.[51]

But civil government could not rely on persuasion. Civil government existed to compel people. And Jefferson did not think that men could live happily without its compulsions. He did once make a rash statement to the effect that if given a choice between having a government and having newspapers, he would prefer newspapers.[52] But that was before he got a full taste of how low newspapers could sink. And though he was fascinated by the government of the American Indians, which relied almost wholly on the weight of public opinion as a means of compulsion,[53] he was not so visionary as to think that this would be a sufficient means for other Americans. The people of the United States needed government. It must be a limited government, allowing every possible liberty to the individual. But it must be strong enough to protect that liberty not only from Americans who sought to exploit their countrymen but also from foreign nations with the same bent. External threats to American freedom and independence loomed as large for Jefferson as they did for Adams and Washington. And here again Jefferson perceived the problem as one of escape from the tyranny of the past.

Jefferson's first venture into foreign affairs was an assault on the ancient mercantilist system by which the governments of the Western world strangled freedom of trade. In the year of American independence Adam Smith had pointed out in *The Wealth of Nations* how the regulation of commerce by the governments of Europe worked against the interests of the people they governed. It was a mercantilist system, he said, because it was dominated by merchants rather than producers, who constituted the vast majority of the population and were the only source of a nation's true wealth. It was a system designed, in the case of England, not for a nation of shopkeepers but for a nation whose government was dominated by its shopkeepers. Jefferson was in full agreement. As a member of Congress he helped to draft a commercial policy of free trade for the United States and then went to Europe to try to achieve the policy through commercial treaties. The objective was to give America's farmers new outlets for their produce by removing the merchant-inspired barriers through which European governments were hampering the happiness of their own peoples under the pretext of helping it.[54]

The experience was a chastening one. It probably helped to establish Jefferson's doubts that people could win freedom suddenly in countries bound by vested interests to the tyranny of the past. When Jefferson found it impossible to achieve his larger goal of opening trade with all Europe, he concentrated on France and there gained a limited success in breaking down bureaucratic barriers that impeded the sale of American tobacco and whale oil. But within a few years his accomplishment was wiped out when the patriots of the French Revolution proved even more blind to the advantages of free trade than the ancien régime had been.

When Jefferson returned to America he was convinced that European nations must be dealt with according to the rules of the game they were playing, and he was eager to use the power of the new national government to penalize by restrictions the commerce of countries that restricted American trade and shipping. His favored target was England, whose manufactures, with free entry, flooded the American market, while she barred American shipping from her West Indian ports. By discriminatory duties or, if necessary, prohibitions, Jefferson hoped to speak to the British in the only language he thought they would heed.[55]

He was defeated in this object by Alexander Hamilton and a crew of American merchants and capitalists who had tied the national government to a British-style fiscal system that seemed to Jefferson to be a betrayal of the Revolution. Hamilton, in fact, professed an admiration for British government and British policies that left Jefferson aghast. By the time Washington's second term was up, Hamilton and the Federalists, in Jefferson's view, had captured the government of the United States, with the intention of fastening all the evils of the past, including monarchy and aristocracy, on independent Americans.

As the federal government turned its face backward, Jefferson counted on the mass of independent farmers to reaffirm their independence. And this they did in the election that made him president, an event that Jefferson liked to call the Revolution of 1800. By that time, however, Hamilton's fiscal system had run up a national debt of $83 million. As president, Jefferson pared away at it and reduced the expenses and activities and offices of government to a minimum, but he was never able to overthrow the old system, and he never gained acceptance of his own most radical scheme to free Americans from the tyrannous grip of the past. Although not adopted or recognized, that scheme embodied a principle that lay at the center of independence for Jefferson. It was the principle, in his own words, that "The Earth belongs in usufruct to the living."[56]

Jefferson first enunciated the principle in France, prompted apparently by discussions with an eccentric English physician and also, no doubt, by the visible evidence all around him of the ways in which ancient laws, customs, and privileges perpetuated ignorance and misery. The idea rested on what he decided was a law of nature, that "one generation is to another as one independant nation to another."[57] But since generations are continuous, he calculated the duration of a generation, from tables of mortality, as the length of time required for a majority of the adult population to die. That period, which he put at about nineteen or twenty years, was the maximum length of time during which any law or constitution could be considered to have the consent of the people on whom it operated and the maximum length of time for which any public debt could rightly be contracted. In explaining the principle to James Madison in 1789, Jefferson was full of hope that the United States might establish it as a matter of fiscal policy. "No nation," he pointed out, "can make a declaration against the validity of long-contracted debts so disinterestedly as we, since we do not owe a shilling which may not be paid with ease, principal and interest, within the time of our own lives."[58] That, alas, was before Alexander Hamilton did his work.

Although Jefferson was never able to undo what Hamilton had done and never attempted to write his natural law into a statute or into the Constitution of the United States or any other state, he did what he could to get the national government on a pay-as-you-go basis. The chief problem, he knew, as well as the chief benefit, would come in relation to war. War was then as now the most expensive activity of government. By the same token it was the principal expense with which one generation could wrongfully saddle its successors. Jefferson was no pacifist, and he knew that war might involve a greater expense than a nation could collect from current revenue, but that fact conferred no right. A government could borrow to pay for a war, but it ought never to do so "without laying a tax in the same instant" for paying the interest annually and the principal within twenty years.[59] If the result would be fewer wars, that was hardly a disadvantage. The result would also be that the people of one generation would not be held in bondage to pay for their predecessors' mistakes and adventures.

Behind Jefferson's right of expatriation from the past lay his conviction that God had created man free and independent and that all institutions of human creation were justifiable only as they helped men to enjoy that birthright. Ideally he would have liked to restructure American society to ensure to the individual a maximum freedom of action. He would have organized men into little republics called hundreds, comprised of people living near enough to meet together. Jefferson's hundreds would have resembled the New England towns which had resulted from the early Congregationalists' insistence that a church must be composed of people living close enough to worship together. Jefferson did not think that God required this kind of community worship, but he did think that human God-given independence would benefit from keeping as many of the powers of government as possible in the hands of men who were able to assemble regularly in their own neighborhoods to govern themselves. In these small units the individual could make his needs and wishes felt directly, and they could accordingly be trusted with more authority than should be allowed to the larger units of government, in which men would have to delegate powers to representatives. The larger units could include those that already existed: counties, states, and finally the national government, whose remoteness from the individual made it most in need of limitation.[60]

Jefferson had first proposed such a restructuring of society and government in his revisal of the Virginia laws, and he continued to propound it in later years. But he had no greater success in winning others to it than he had with his proposals for limiting the national debt. His countrymen remained more bound to the past than he, and he never supposed that he could extricate them from it more rapidly than they were ready to move. As president of the United States he knew that it was his duty to act for them, to see farther than they did, but not to mistake his own predilection for theirs. He often acted more vigorously and aggressively in their behalf than his predecessors in the presidential chair had done. But he never confused the end with the means as both of them sometimes did. In the eyes of Thomas Jefferson it was not for the government, whether state or national, to tell the people what they wanted. Government was a means to an end, a means to protect and preserve the sacred freedom of the individual; and in the last analysis even the nation was no more than a means to that end.

For Jefferson, as for John Adams and George Washington, independence brought a kind of personal fulfillment. His was a different, less apparent fulfillment than they enjoyed, but it was similarly rooted in a personal trait. Jefferson, as I have stated, was a very private man. Although he did not cultivate the kind of aloofness with which Washington held others at somewhat more than arm's length, he possessed an inner core of personal privacy that no one has ever breached. His privacy, I believe, was a symptom of the supreme value he placed on individual freedom. It was not mere seclusion that he valued; he might have enjoyed far greater privacy of that sort by not participating in the Revolution at all. But in the establishment of independent republican government in America, Jefferson saw an opportunity to enlarge for mankind the private world in which the individual reigns supreme. The Revolution he fought was for the right of the individual to manage his own life with the minimum of interference from governments. For him the triumph of independence meant the triumph of the individual.

Thomas Jefferson had his limitations. We may rightly take him to task (and George Washington as well) for not concerning himself with individuals who happened to be black. We may chide him too for thinking that politics and learning were purely masculine pursuits. But he would have been the first to pronounce his hope and expectation that subsequent generations would expand the dimensions of independence, dimensions hidden to him, for both men and women, white and black. For his own part he concentrated on what was not hidden from him, on what he thought possible, on what he thought Americans were ready for: equal treatment for westerners with easterners, and for younger sons with older sons, freedom for every man to worship or not worship as he pleased, a general lightening of the load of government that men had hitherto borne. Without Adams's ambition or Washington's thirst for honor, he found in independence a humbler yet deeper meaning. He too was a great American, but above all he was a friend of man.

1. Julian P. Boyd, ed., *The Papers of Thomas Jefferson* (Princeton, N.J., 1950–), vols. 17–19, passim, especially the longer headnotes to the various documents relating to foreign relations. All quotations from Jefferson dated before Jan. 25, 1791, are from this work, hereafter referred to simply as Boyd. Quotations and references after this date are either from *The Writings of Thomas Jefferson*, ed. Paul L. Ford (New York, 1892–99), hereafter referred to as Ford, or from *The Writings of Thomas Jefferson*, ed. Andrew A. Lipscomb and Albert E. Bergh (Washington, D.C., 1903–4), hereafter referred to as L and B. The definitive biographical works are Dumas Malone, *Jefferson and His Time* (Boston, 1948–), and Merrill D. Peterson, *Thomas Jefferson and the New Nation* (New York, 1970). An excellent selection of Jefferson's writings is Peterson, *The Portable Thomas Jefferson* (New York, 1975).

2. L and B, 1:324.

3. L and B, 1:358, 376.

4. To William Plumer, Jan. 31, 1815, to Lafayette, Feb. 14, 1815, L and B, 14:235–37, 247.

5. To John Dickinson, Jan. 13, 1807, to John Holmes, April 22, 1820, to Lafayette, Dec. 26, 1820, to William Short, Sept. 8, 1823, Ford, 9:8; L and B, 15:249–50, 299–302, 469. On Jefferson and slavery, see William Cohen, "Thomas Jefferson and the Problem of Slavery," *Journal of American History* 56 (1969):503–26; David B. Davis, *Was Thomas Jefferson an Authentic Enemy of Slavery?* (Oxford, 1970); Winthrop D. Jordan, *White over Black: American Attitudes toward the Negro, 1550–1812* (Chapel Hill, N.C., 1968), pp. 429–81; and E. S. Morgan, *American Slavery, American Freedom: The Ordeal of Colonial Virginia* (New York, 1975), pp. 374–87.

6. May 11, 1788, Boyd, 13:151. See also to same, Feb. 7, 1787, Boyd, 11:122–23.

7. Sept. 21, 1788, Boyd, 13:623.

8. To Albert Gallatin, Jan. 13, 1807, Ford, 9:7.

9. To Elizabeth Wayles Eppes, Oct. 31, 1790, Boyd, 17:658.

10. Feb. 2, 1791, Boyd, 19:239.

11. See, for example, to James Madison, Feb. 20, April 25, 1784, Boyd, 6:548–49, 7:119.

12. Boyd, 8:230–32, 266–67, 483–85, 9:188.

13. Boyd, 7:511–12, 639, 8:418, 9:168, 10:86, 123–25, 176–78, 224–25, 486, 560–70, 13:500.

14. To James Monroe, Aug. 11, 1786, Boyd, 10:225.

15. Oct. 3, 1785, Boyd, 8:580.

16. To John Adams, July 11, 1786, from John Adams, July 31, 1786, Boyd, 10:123–25, 176–78.

17. Boyd, 18:369–416.

18. To Archibald Stuart, Jan. 25, 1786, Boyd, 9:218.

19. Ibid. and to William Carmichael, June 3, 1788, Boyd, 13:231.

20. To Archibald Stuart, Jan. 25, 1786, to James Monroe, Aug. 11, 1786, to James Madison, Jan. 30, 1787, to William Carmichael, Sept. 29, 1787, to John Melish, Dec. 31, 1816, Boyd, 9:218, 10:223–25, 11:93–94, 12:173, and L and B, 15:93–95.

21. John A. Logan, Jr., *No Transfer: An American Security Principle* (New Haven, 1961); Ford, 9:212–13.

22. To Destutt de Tracy, Jan. 26, 1811, L and B, 13:18.

23. To C. W. F. Dumas, Nov. 14, 1787, Boyd, 12:360.

24. L and B, 1:330, 9:7, 36–40, 114–17.

25. To Charles Bellini, Sept. 30, 1785, Boyd, 8:568–69.

26. To James Madison, Jan. 30, 1787, to John Rutledge, Aug. 6, 1787, Boyd, 11:93, 701. Jefferson's phrase is actually "kites" over pigeons; kites are more commonly seen than other types of hawks in many parts of Europe.

27. Aug. 13, 1786, Boyd, 10:244.

28. Boyd, 11:186, 227–28, 14:212–13, 15:165–68, 230–33, L and B, 1:139–40.

29. To M. de Neufville, Dec. 13, 1818, L and B, 15:175–77.

30. To Lafayette, Feb. 14, 1815, L and B, 14:245–46.

31. L and B, 13:40, 14:21, 15:114–18.

32. To Joseph Priestley, Nov. 29, 1802, Ford, 8:179.

33. To David Humphreys, Aug. 14, 1787, Boyd, 12:33.

34. To James Monroe, July 9, 1786, Boyd, 10:112. See also Boyd, 10:603, 11:93–94.

35. To John C. Breckenridge, Aug. 12, 1803, Ford, 8:243–44.

36. Boyd, 1:121, 18:311, 311n.

37. To William Carmichael and William Short, April 24, 1792, L and B, 8:326–34.

38. To Ezra Stiles, Dec. 24, 1786, to James Madison, Jan. 30, 1787, Boyd, 10:629, 11:93.

39. Boyd, 16:330n, 451n, 17:341n, 472n, 638–39, 645, 18:491–92.

40. *Notes on the State of Virginia*, ed. William Peden (Chapel Hill, N.C., 1955), pp. 164–65.

41. Aristotle, *Politics*, Book VI; James Harrington, *The Commonwealth of Oceana* (London, 1656).

42. J. G. A. Pocock, "Machiavelli, Harrington, and English Political Ideologies in the Eighteenth Century," *William and Mary Quarterly*, 3d ser., 22 (1965): 549–83, at p. 567.

43. *Notes on Virginia*, pp. 84–85.

44. For various expressions of Jefferson's view of the necessarily slow pace of progress, see Ford, 8:341–48, and L and B, 13:40, 14:20–25, 245–46, 296–97, 15:114, 16:74–75, 289, 434.

45. Ford, 8:345.
46. To Henry Lee, Aug. 10, 1824, Ford, 10:317.
47. Boyd, 2:305–665; *Notes on Virginia,* pp. 130–49.
48. L and B, 1:256–59; C. R. Keim, "Primogeniture and Entail in Colonial Virginia," *William and Mary Quarterly,* 3d ser., 25 (1968): 545–86.
49. To Edmund Randolph, Aug. 18, 1799, to Charles Pinckney, Oct. 29, 1799, to John Tyler, June 17, 1812, Ford, 7:383–87, 397–99, and L and B, 13:165–68.
50. "Jefferson's Hints to Americans Travelling in Europe," Boyd, 12:272. See also to Mrs. M. H. Smith, Aug. 6, 1816, L and B, 15:60: "My opinion is that there would never have been an infidel, if there had never been a priest."
51. To Jeremiah Moore, Aug. 14, 1800, Ford, 7:454–55.
52. To Edward Carrington, Jan. 16, 1787, Boyd, 11:49.
53. To Francis W. Gilmer, June 7, 1816, L and B, 15:25–26.
54. Merrill D. Peterson, "Thomas Jefferson and Commercial Policy, 1783–1793," *William and Mary Quarterly,* 3d ser., 22 (1965): 584–610.
55. Boyd, 17:35–108, 18:220–306, 516–77, 19:543, 558–75; L and B, 8:216–23, 9:34, 75–78, 87–89, 138–39, 373.
56. Boyd, 15:384–99; L and B, 13:269–79, 353–68, 15:41–43.
57. To James Madison, Sept. 6, 1789, Boyd, 15:395.
58. Ibid., p. 397.
59. To John W. Eppes, June 24, 1813, L and B, 13:269.
60. Boyd, 2:526–35; L and B, 1:122, 14:47, 84, 419–23, 490–91, 15:18–23, 32–43. Jefferson put the idea most succinctly and eloquently in a letter to Joseph C. Cabell, Feb. 2, 1816: "It is by dividing and subdividing these republics from the great national one down through all its subordinations, until it ends in the administration of every man's farm by himself; by placing under every one what his own eye may superintend, that all will be done for the best. What has destroyed liberty and the rights of man in every government which has ever existed under the sun? The generalizing and concentrating all cares and powers into one body, no matter whether of the autocrats of Russia or France, or of the aristocrats of a Venetian senate. And I do believe that if the Almighty has not decreed that man shall never be free, (and it is a blasphemy to believe it,) that the secret will be found to be in the making himself the depository of the powers respecting himself, so far as he is competent to them, and delegating only what is beyond his competence by a synthetical process, to higher and higher orders of functionaries, so as to trust fewer and fewer powers in proportion as the trustees become more and more oligarchical" (L and B, 14:421–22).

INDEX

slavery, 64, 74
slaves, 33–34, 38
Smith, Adam, 80
Spain, 45, 53, 68, 71
Stamp Act, 3, 13

tobacco, 80
Tufts, Cotton, 21

Virginia, 38–39, 43, 44–46, 66

Warren, James, 45
Washington, George: appointment of, 18; aloofness of, 31–32, 37–38, 49, 52; and Mount Vernon, 32–35; and slaves, 33–34, 38; and overseers, 34; and agriculture, 35; and vanity, 36; and military rank, 37; and republicanism, 39–40, 47, 55; and Congress, 39–42, 46–47; and French, 42; and union, 42–48; and Society of the Cincinnati, 44; and immigration, 44–45, 50–51; and West, 44–45, 50–51, 52–53; and rebellion, 46–47; and Constitutional Convention, 47–48; and presidency, 48–49; and foreign relations, 49–54
Washington, Lawrence, 36
West Indies, 46, 80
whale oil, 80
Wigglesworth, Michael, 11
Winthrop, John, 11
Wythe, George, 71
women, 64–65

Young, Arthur, 36